praise for Magic Johnson's *What YOU can do to avoid AIDS*

"Today the most important gift a parent can give a child is a frank conversation about AIDS. That means taking the time to listen to our children's concerns and having the facts we need to tell them how to survive the age of AIDS. With this book, Magic Johnson offers an invaluable tool for starting that conversation and for helping teens understand what everyone needs to know about AIDS."

—Mathilde Krim, Ph.D.
Chairman, American Foundation for AIDS Research (AmFAR)

"AIDS is a preventable disease, but only if we are educated. Magic has a special glow. His smile and honesty can reach many and help save countless lives. His shoes are big, but believe me—you don't want to be in them. Pay attention now, not later. His is a message of life and hope."

—Elizabeth Glaser
Co-Founder, Pediatric AIDS Foundation

"This outstanding book is by far the most honest, straightforward, and explicit HIV prevention guide written for teens. The courage, honesty, and strength Magic has shown in dealing with being HIV-infected shine through in this book, making it a much-needed, powerful, and frank message to teens and adults."

—National Network of Runaway and Youth Services

Earvin "MAGIC" Johnson

what you can do to avoid AIDS

TIMES BOOKS

RANDOM HOUSE

*To my friend Elizabeth Glaser
(1947–1994), for all the help she gave me
personally. I have been inspired by her
strength and willpower and all the
battles she fought for people who have
HIV and AIDS*

ISBN: 0-8129-2844-X

Books are available at special discounts for bulk
purchases (100 copies or more) for sales promotions or
premiums. Special editions, including personalized
covers, can be created in large quantities for special
needs. For more information write to Special
Marketing, 201 East 50th Street, New York, NY 10022,
or call 1-800-800-3246.

Manufactured in the United States of America

Designed by Beth Tondreau Design
Illustrations by Robert P. D. Scudellari

9 8 7 6 5 4 3 2
First Edition

contents

introduction to the new edition

A few months ago I did something I never thought I'd have the opportunity to do again: return to the NBA and play for the Los Angeles Lakers. I retired from professional basketball in November, 1991, after I discovered I'd been infected with HIV, the virus that causes AIDS. I attempted a comeback in 1992, but again had to walk away from the game I love when players were afraid they'd be infected by the virus.

Significant changes have taken place in the last four years. Thanks to education and awareness, we are finally understanding that you don't have to fear people with HIV. That's one of the reasons I'm back on the court—the knowledge that you don't get HIV from casual contact.

That's the good news. The bad news is that there is still no cure for HIV or AIDS. Despite everything we know we can do to keep the virus from spreading, more and more people are getting infected. Today, there are 19 to 20 million people who are HIV-positive, up from an estimated 12 million in 1992. Although new and promising treatments have come along, 40 percent of the 19 to 20 million people infected will probably develop AIDS within nine years. As far as we know, AIDS is fatal. It killed my friend Elizabeth Glaser, and it could kill someone you love.

When I read how attitudes toward people with HIV are changing, I know at least part of the message is getting through. At the same time, I worry that everyone will think, "Well, good, the panic's over. I don't need to worry about AIDS anymore because it can't happen to me." Think again! In the four years since I wrote the first edition of this book, over 150,000 Americans have lost their lives to AIDS. If you think it can't happen to you, remember there are 19 to 20 million people who will tell you you're wrong. HIV/AIDS is everyone's problem.

If we're ready to hear the message and take personal responsibility for our actions, we can fight HIV and AIDS. This book can help.

acknowledgments

this book has been a real team effort. I could never have written this book alone. There are so many people and organizations I want to thank.

First and foremost, I want to thank C. Everett Koop, M.D., former surgeon general of the United States. Dr. Koop has been my adviser and consultant from the very beginning of this project. He pointed me in the direction of other experts I have relied on in trying to get my message out to kids with accuracy and sensitivity.

I also want to express my deepest gratitude to the many others who have lent their advice, expertise, and recommendations to the project: Jay Coburn, Director, Safe Choices Project, the National Network of Runaway and Youth Services, Inc.; Rebecca Denison, founder of *World,* a monthly newsletter for women who are HIV positive; the late Elizabeth Glaser, cofounder of the Pediatric AIDS Foundation; Mathilde Krim, Ph.D., Chair, American Foundation for AIDS Research (AmFAR); Ann Northrop, who has educated many teens about HIV; Karen J. Peterson, Ph.D., American Red Cross National Headquarters, Office of HIV/AIDS Education; the Reverend Margaret Reinfeld, Director of Education, AmFAR; and Mary Jane Rotheram-Borus, Ph.D., who has done outstanding research on teen runaways and HIV.

Special thanks go to Debbie Bial, Director of the College Posse Scholarship Program, Lynn Gray, President, metaNetworks, Inc., Sandy Gutierrez, Director of the Leadership Training Institute, and the metaNetworks "brain trust"—Ingrid Anne Boutin, Melissa Delacruz, Hassan Elgendi, Kito Huggins, Chanrithy Ouk, and Eli Saposnick. The teenagers and counselors at metaNetworks helped shape the manuscript tremendously. They not only helped me figure out how to get my message across to teenagers, but they read and critiqued the manuscript. I'm grateful for your generosity.

A number of individuals and organizations have graciously allowed me to include material from their publications. The Centers for Disease Control and Prevention provided statistics on the number of cases of AIDS in the United States and shared its guidelines for the use of condoms in helping prevent the spread of HIV. Planned Parenthood of New York City and Planned Parenthood® Federation of America, Inc., shared information on sexually transmitted diseases and birth control devices, which appears in Chapter 4. Keith Hefner, Executive Director, gave me permission to reprint two articles from *New Youth Connections*, an excellent magazine in New York City for teens written by teens, in chapters 2 and 3. I want to thank the writers of those articles: Cassaundra Worrell ("So You're Scared to Buy Rubbers? So Was I") and Kyeeniah Nix ("You Don't Want to Have Sex? You're Not Alone"). The Children's Defense Fund gave me permission to reprint material from "Teens and AIDS: Opportunities for Prevention." Chelsea Psychotherapy Associates gave me permission to adapt their suggestions for how to help people with HIV/AIDS, which are revised from the original written by Dixie Beckham, Diego Lopez, Luis Palacios-Jimenez, Vincent John Patti, and Michael Shernoff.

The profiles of Antigone, Dawn Marcal, and S.T. were reprinted with permission from *WORLD*, a Northern California newsletter by, for, and about women facing HIV disease. Persons who wish to contact the newsletter can write to Rebecca Denison, WORLD, P.O. Box 11535, Oakland, CA 94611, or call (510) 658-6930.

Special thanks to The Learning Partnership for permission to reprint the profile of the late David Kamens, which appears in *Straight Talk: HIV/AIDS and Other STDs*, a magazine for teenagers.

I'm very grateful to the people and organizations who reviewed and commented on the manuscript: the American Foundation for AIDS Research; the American Medical Association; the American Red Cross; the Children's Defense Fund; Elizabeth Glaser, cofounder of the Pediatric AIDS Foundation; David Kamens; the National Community AIDS Partnership; the National Network of Runaway and Youth Services; the National Runaway Switchboard; Ann Northrop; Philip A. Pizzo, M.D., Chief, Pediatric Branch, and Head, Infectious Disease Section of the National Cancer Institute; Planned Parenthood of New York City; and Planned Parenthood® Federation of America, Inc.

I also want to thank all the people with HIV/AIDS who have shared their stories: Antigone, Bill Drumright, Joe B. Franco, Elizabeth Glaser, David Kamens, Dawn Marcal, and S.T. Thanks for your courage and inspiration.

Finally, many thanks to all the folks at Times Books and Random House who made this book happen. And I'd like to particularly thank my editor, Betsy Rapoport.

caution

You're going to read some very frank things about sex in this book. Sometimes I use words you'll hear more often in the locker room than in the classroom. I do so because it's important that every reader —especially young people—understand exactly what I'm talking about. I'm not trying to offend anyone. I'm trying to educate everyone in the best—and most direct—way possible.

a note about medical advice

This book is not meant to be a substitute for the advice of a doctor or professional health-care worker. In fact, one of the important messages I want to share with you is that if you are sexually active or are thinking of becoming sexually active, you should talk with a doctor or professional health-care worker who can help you make the best decisions about your health. You should **never** try to diagnose or treat yourself; doing so can be very dangerous, since you might not get the right treatment when you need it. It's your body; work with your doctor or health-care worker as a team to keep it healthy.

a message from Earvin "MAGIC" Johnson

On November 7, 1991, I retired from professional basketball because a blood test showed I was infected with HIV, the virus that causes AIDS.

I got the results of my HIV antibody test less than two months after I'd married my college sweetheart, Cookie, and less than seven weeks after she and I learned she was pregnant. Those few weeks before the test results were full of unbelievable joy for us. We'd finally decided to spend the rest of our lives together. We were starting the family we'd wanted for so long. And then, boom, everything changed—forever. Because of my infection, I had unknowingly put Cookie and our unborn child at risk, too. Fortunately, my wife has tested negative for the virus.

Many people have called me a hero because I've chosen to dedicate the rest of my life to educating people—especially teenagers—about HIV and how to protect themselves from it. But let me be clear about one thing: I'm not a hero because I got HIV. And I didn't get HIV because I was a "bad" person or a "dirty" one or someone who "deserved" it for whatever reason. No one "deserves" to get HIV. I got HIV because I had unprotected sex. I got HIV because I thought HIV could never happen to someone like me. Obviously, if I could turn the clock back, I would have acted differently. But I can't. I can only go forward. With the love and support of my family and friends, I'm going to fight this illness as best I can. And pass on to you the lessons I have learned the hard way.

I have been very fortunate since I told the world that I have HIV. Although some people have said and written some unkind things about me since I went public with my terrible news, in general people have accepted me and most of them tell me they still love me. But I'm one of the lucky ones. Most people with HIV infection, including AIDS, don't get that kind of support. They are rejected, sometimes even by family

2

and friends. That rejection is one of the worst things about having the infection.

Discrimination is ugly. It's based on hate and ignorance. Too many of us know what it feels like to be discriminated against because of our color or religion or disability or sexual identity. People with HIV are discriminated against, too. There's discrimination based on hate: A lot of people who should know better say that AIDS is something that gay people "brought on themselves." Or that people who get HIV by sharing contaminated needles are "just druggies getting what's coming to them." Or that "if she hadn't been sleeping around, she wouldn't have gotten AIDS." There's discrimination based on ignorance: Some people are so scared they even refuse to shake hands with me. They don't understand how you get the virus, and they think you can catch HIV the same way you catch a cold. I've even heard of doctors, dentists, and nurses refusing to care for people who have HIV or who have developed AIDS. People who are infected sometimes lose their jobs, their homes, their friends. Some families even desert their own child if he or she gets HIV. That means when you're fighting for your life—when you most need the help of your friends and family—you might have to fight the loneliest fight of all.

Let's get it straight—and you'll hear me talk about this again and again—AIDS is not about "us" and "them." People don't get HIV because they're "bad," and people are not protected because they're "good." **You don't get HIV because of who you are—you get it because of what you do.** We're all at risk. Everybody who has HIV or who has developed AIDS deserves our support and compassion. Let's put a stop to the hate and fear.

Since I learned I had HIV, I've heard a lot of talk about who's a hero and who's a role model. I've been learning everything I can about HIV and AIDS, and my heroes—my role models—are the people who are educating others about this terrible disease, people who show love and compassion and caring for the people who have it.

I intend to dedicate myself to making the public, and especially young people, more aware of HIV and AIDS—what the virus is, how it's spread, and how you can avoid it so what happened to me will never happen to you. Education and the courage to change risky behaviors are our best weapons against HIV.

The first thing we have to do is stop the denial— denial that HIV is out there, denial that says, "It can't happen to me." Believe me, I know what denial is all about. It wasn't so much that I didn't have informa- tion about HIV and AIDS. It was right there in my face—on the radio and TV, in newspapers and maga- zines. The L.A. Lakers even had lectures on HIV in the locker room. I wish I had paid attention. I just didn't think it could ever happen to me. Until we accept that anybody can get HIV, the epidemic is go- ing to continue to grow. Throughout this book you'll find profiles of people with HIV. They'll help you see that this virus touches us all.

Don't put your head in the sand. Anyone can get HIV. But knowledge is power, and that's what this book is all about. I want to give you the education, skills, and support to protect yourself (and others)—not only against HIV but also against other sexually transmitted diseases and unwanted pregnancy. I want you to understand the connection between HIV and drug use. I want to help you learn to be a sexually responsible person and to take charge of your own life.

Random House, Inc., will be donating all of the net profits from this book directly to the Magic Johnson Foundation, which I started to support HIV/AIDS education, prevention, and care. We desperately need more information about causes and cures. If you want to write me or send a donation, please contact:

Magic Johnson Foundation
1888 Century Park East
Suite 310
Los Angeles, CA 90067
Telephone: (310) 785–0201

I'm very grateful for the incredible support I've received from all over the world, even from people who have criticized some of the things I've done. I hope we can learn to give the same support to all people with HIV, no matter how they got it.

Please read this book and share it with the people you love. If we stop the ignorance, we can stop AIDS.

a message to
parents

in an ideal world, parents would teach their growing children all about love and sex. But most of us learn from friends and TV and movies. And these days, with a deadly virus running loose, that's dangerous because there's too much wrong information out there. So please talk to your kids. Parents are the key to preventing HIV.

Your job is tougher now than it ever was. When

your son or daughter gets to a certain age, you'll look at your watch and think, "Time for that talk about the birds and the bees." But now you'll also have to talk about HIV and AIDS. Take your child aside and say, "We love you and don't want anything bad to happen to you. We'd like you not to have sexual intercourse until you're ready to be responsible about it. But someday you will be sexually active, so we want you to be prepared. Let us make sure you have the facts about how to protect yourself and others."

Teach your kids the value of abstinence. They need to understand that postponing sexual intercourse is a sensible option with rewards that go far beyond freedom from AIDS, unwanted pregnancy, or sexually transmitted diseases. I've certainly emphasized that in this book. It's not enough to say to your child, "No sex," or, "You can't," because, like it or not, it's your child who will decide when he or she is ready. You must therefore also teach your kids about **safer** sex.

If you've built trust with your kids, they'll know they can come to you with their questions. If they bring up the subject of sex or sexuality or sexual identity, don't panic. And please try not to judge them— even if you have strong feelings on the matter. The most important thing we can do to protect our kids' lives is to listen to their questions and to give them the honest, straightforward information they need and want.

When you talk about HIV and AIDS, one of the issues that's going to come up is homosexuality. Many

homosexuality is a sexual orientation

of you may have been raised to believe that homosexuality is unnatural or morally wrong. In fact, homosexuality is a sexual orientation that you have, not one that you choose. And please remember: Your kids live in a world where, like it or not, there are people who feel more attracted to others of their own sex than to the opposite sex. Many experts believe that 10 percent of the population is gay and lesbian. Your children need clear information. Give it to them. And then tell them about your values. Understand that at this time in their lives they may challenge your beliefs. That's natural.

It is heartbreaking beyond words when parents reject their own children because those children happen to be gay or lesbian. If a gay child gets the message that being gay is somehow a bad thing, he or she may see HIV infection as a kind of punishment that's deserved, and he or she might not even bother to try to protect himself or herself—or others.

Your values are your business, of course, and I'm not writing this book to get into a debate with you about homosexuality. Many people have been taught that homosexuality is a sin. If that has been your upbringing, remember that the very same religious teachings also tell us that we are all sinners and are obligated to give the same loving attention to others that we would want for ourselves. You should also know that more and more religious leaders and congregations support lesbian and gay people. I am asking you to give your kids a sense that we are all God's creatures and that we all deserve love and compassion.

Like most teenagers, your kid may be embarrassed, shy, or unwilling to listen when you bring up these subjects. I know how hard it can be to talk to your kids. But stick with it. This education takes time. It's one of the most valuable gifts you'll ever give your child.

Don't wait for your kids to ask about sex. Kids are smarter than parents think they are. They know what's happening. Talk to them early, before they're faced with decisions about their sexuality. Talk to them in their language. Don't scare them. Then maintain that open atmosphere for communication. That's how I talk to my son, Andre. If your kids do come to you to tell you that they've been sexually active or are thinking about it, be there to help. Tell them you're proud of them for having the courage to bring the subject up or for wanting to know how to protect themselves. If you sense that your children aren't comfortable talking with you about sex, homosexuality, or HIV/AIDS, or if you can't give them the information they need, give them the name of a school counselor or a health-care provider or a member of the clergy they can talk with.

Remember to talk to your kids about drugs, too. Make sure they know the facts about drugs and HIV.

Stay involved in your children's lives. Don't miss the chance to talk with your kids about what's important.

10

CHAPTER 1
what are
HIV and
AIDS?

You've probably been hearing a lot about HIV infection and AIDS. What you've heard may have scared you. But being scared won't help you make wise choices about your health. Being educated will. Let me lay out the basics here so you'll understand what HIV and AIDS are and how HIV is—and isn't—spread. I'll start with two simple definitions.

what's the difference between HIV and AIDS?

HIV stands for *human immunodeficiency virus*. What do those words mean? Let's break them down.

Human means human beings, not animals, plants, or insects.

Immuno refers to the immune system, the organs and cells that fight off diseases and infection in our bodies.

Deficiency means a breakdown or lack of something, so *immunodeficiency* means the immune system is damaged and can't function properly to fight off infections or diseases very well.

Virus is an extremely tiny germ able to cause diseases. Certain viruses, such as HIV, can enter the cells of your body and prevent them from doing what they're supposed to do.

HIV is a virus that can be spread from person to person in specific ways and can cause an infected person's immune system to break down or collapse completely. **HIV is the virus that causes AIDS.**

AIDS stands for *acquired immunodeficiency syndrome*. What do those words mean? Again, let's break them down:

Acquired means you're not born with it, but can develop it later.

Immunodeficiency means your immune system is damaged and can't function properly to fight off infections or diseases.

HIV is the virus that causes Acquired

Syndrome means a combination of physical signs and symptoms.

Let's look at this like a war. There are parts of your blood that—like an army—are called in to fight the enemy, disease. The main soldiers in your immune system are white blood cells. They attack the viruses, bacteria, and other foreign agents that from time to time invade your body. Normally, your white blood cells destroy these invaders and keep you from getting infections or diseases. When HIV enters your body, however, it heads right for the white blood cells and takes *them* over. As the virus multiplies, it kills white blood cells, destroying your body's defenses. When this happens, you become a target for diseases and infections that healthy people can usually fight off easily.

These "opportunistic" infections include *pneumocystis carinii* pneumonia, tuberculosis, yeast infections, and other infections. You are also vulnerable to certain cancers, such as Kaposi's sarcoma, a rare form of cancer. When you have HIV and have developed certain infections, doctors say you have AIDS. (This is why AIDS is called a "syndrome" and not a "disease.") People do not die of AIDS; they die because the virus makes their bodies so weak that they can't fight off the opportunistic illnesses.

HIV and AIDS are not the same thing

Three things first:

▶ HIV is the virus that causes the condition of AIDS.
▶ You can't "catch" AIDS, but you **can** get infected with HIV, the virus that causes AIDS.
▶ Being infected with HIV doesn't mean you automatically have AIDS. For the majority of people, however, it means that, sooner or later, you will develop AIDS.

If you become infected with HIV, the virus can live inside your body for ten years or longer before you show any symptoms. During that time you may look and feel healthy, but you can infect others with the virus. **In other words: You can get the virus without knowing it. You can pass it on to others without you or your partner knowing it. In fact, most people who have HIV don't even know they're infected.**

One basic way a doctor can make a sure diagnosis of HIV infection is by an **HIV antibody test** (sometimes called the "AIDS test"—see below). **You can't tell whether someone has HIV or AIDS just by looking at him or her—not even if you're a doctor.** Even if the test says you've got HIV antibodies, you do not necessarily have AIDS. Only a doctor or qualified health worker can tell you whether you also have AIDS—and only after he or she has given you a complete physical examination and done lab tests.

HIV infection is a **progressive condition.** That means you start off by getting infected with HIV, then later on you will probably get sick. "Later on" could mean weeks, months, or many years. After you begin to show symptoms, there may be times when you feel terrific and times when you feel terribly sick. You can go back and forth between feeling healthy and feeling sick many times, but as your immune system becomes more damaged and less able to fight off disease, you will find it more and more difficult to get better when you do get sick. This is because HIV is destroying more and more of your white blood cells. This makes it harder for your immune system to fight off illnesses, even with the help of medicines such as antibiotics. Eventually, you'll have no more defenses. The opportunistic illnesses could make you so sick that you could die.

is there a cure?
No, not yet. So far, there is no cure for HIV infection. Scientists do not know if everyone who is HIV-infected will develop AIDS. Most will. Many live for years after being diagnosed with AIDS. If you're diagnosed soon after you get infected with HIV and you get into treatment, your chances of living longer are better, because there are medications you can take to help keep you healthy and possibly postpone the development of AIDS.

how do you catch HIV? and how does it spread?

HIV is a sexually transmitted disease (STD). This means you can get it by having unprotected sexual intercourse with someone who is infected. You can also get it through blood-to-blood contact with an infected person. You already know that HIV infects white blood cells. Most white blood cells are found in two body fluids: **blood** and **semen** (the fluid in which sperm and white blood cells live). But there are also large amounts of HIV-infected white blood cells in the **vaginal fluids** (including menstrual blood) and **breast milk** of someone who is HIV-infected. HIV can be spread when blood, semen, or vaginal fluids from an infected person get into the body of another person. **This can happen in four basic ways.** I'll list them and then talk more about each one.

1) You can get HIV by having unprotected sex—vaginal, anal, or oral intercourse—with someone who is infected. (Throughout this book, when I talk about "having sex," I'm referring to sexual intercourse.)

2) You can get HIV by sharing a needle or "works"—cookers, etc.—with someone who is infected.

3) You can get HIV by getting a blood transfusion or organ transplant from someone who is infected (rare since blood screening began in 1985).

4) A pregnant woman infected with HIV can pass the virus to her child before or after birth.

16

1) You can get HIV by having unprotected vaginal, anal, or oral intercourse (sex) with someone who is infected.

Vaginal intercourse—vaginal sex—is when a man puts his penis into a woman's vagina.

Anal intercourse—anal sex—is when a man puts his penis into the anus (asshole) of a woman or another man.

Oral intercourse—oral sex—is when a woman or a man sucks on or licks a man's penis; or when a man or a woman licks a woman's vaginal area; or when a man or a woman licks another man's or woman's anus —a practice sometimes called "rimming."

Unprotected means having any type of intercourse without the use of a *latex* condom (also called a rubber or a prophylactic).

The vagina, the rectum (the tube that connects the anus and the lower intestine), the hole in the tip of the penis (urethra), the mouth, and the throat are all lined with layers of spongy cells called mucous membranes. (If you run your finger along the inside of your mouth, the slimy lining you feel is a mucous membrane.) Underneath the mucous membranes are blood vessels. When someone has unprotected vaginal, anal, or oral sex, the HIV in the infected person's blood, semen, or vaginal fluids can get soaked up into these mucous membranes just like water is absorbed by a sponge. From there, the virus can get into the other person's bloodstream. Sometimes the rubbing of the penis or tongue against the mucous membranes in the vagina, rectum, or mouth can rub off some of the lining and make tiny tears in the blood vessels so they bleed a little bit. This can happen without either sexual partner knowing it or seeing any blood. Sometimes the openings can already be present in the mucous membranes before intercourse. These little tears make it even easier for the virus in the semen, vaginal fluids, or blood of one partner to get into the other person's bloodstream.

The lining of the vagina is made of many layers of mucous membrane, and the blood vessels there lie deeply below the surface. In the rectum, however, the mucous membrane lining is very thin and the blood vessels are right underneath it, very close to the surface. Unlike the vagina, the rectum doesn't stretch very easily. When you have anal sex, it's easier for HIV to pass into the bloodstream through its thinner mucous membrane lining and it's easier to rip the lining. You may not see any blood after having anal sex, but there are almost always tiny rips. The HIV in the infected man's semen can make its way through these rips into his partner's bloodstream. **Unprotected anal sex is probably the most risky kind of sex.**

The more people you have unprotected sex with, the greater your chances of encountering an infected partner. It's true that some people who have unprotected sex with others infected with HIV don't get the virus. Yet it's also true that **you can get HIV from having unprotected vaginal, anal,**

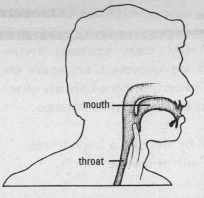

Mucous membranes line the mouth, throat, urethra, rectum, and vagina. HIV in an infected person's blood, semen, or vaginal fluids can get soaked up into these mucous membranes during unprotected vaginal, anal, or oral sex. From there, HIV can get into the uninfected person's bloodstream.

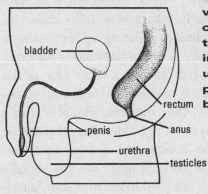

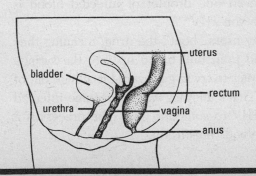

19

or oral sex only once with an infected person.

Remember: HIV can spread from man to woman or woman to man or man to man or woman to woman during unprotected sexual intercourse.

2) You can get HIV by sharing a hypodermic needle or "works" with someone who is infected.

People take drugs many ways. One of the most dangerous is to inject a drug with a needle, either intravenously—that is, directly into a vein (also known as using IV drugs, mainlining, shooting up, or making a hit)—or intradermally ("skin-popping"—injecting drugs under the skin but not into a vein). One of the surest ways to get HIV is to share a needle with someone who has the virus. After someone with HIV uses a needle and syringe to shoot up, a tiny drop of infected blood stays inside the needle and syringe. So if you use that same needle and syringe, you are actually shooting that person's infected blood into your bloodstream. And even one droplet of infected blood is enough to give you HIV.

Some drug users "boot" the drug, meaning they mainline it and then pull blood up into the syringe two or three times to try to get every bit of high out of the injection. That's another way to become infected and transmit HIV to someone else. The process is a kind of mini–blood transfusion.

Sharing needles or works for skin-popping can spread HIV in the same way. When you skin-pop, you're also more likely to get infections such as an abscess, which is a swollen area in which pus gathers.

You can also get HIV from sharing other drug "works"—containers or cookers such as spoons or bottle caps, crack pipes, cotton, or water for dissolving drugs or rinsing syringes—with someone who is infected.

In addition, doing any kind of drug, including drinking alcohol, can be risky because when you're high, your judgment may be poor. You might easily forget to use a latex condom during sex or to avoid sharing a needle.

Remember: It doesn't matter what you're shooting in the needle—heroin, cocaine, speed, steroids, insulin, or any other drug. If you share a needle or works with someone who has HIV, you could get infected, too.

It's unlikely but also possible to get HIV if your ears are pierced with the same needle used to pierce the ears of someone infected with HIV. Or you can get HIV in a blood-sharing ritual (in which two people make small cuts in their fingers and press those fingers together, as you might do when joining a gang). You could also get HIV if you're tattooed with the same needle—or razor or piece of glass—used to tattoo someone who's infected with HIV, especially if blood is drawn in the process.

When someone with HIV uses a needle and syringe to shoot up, a tiny drop of infected blood stays inside the needle and syringe. If you use that same needle and syringe, you are actually shooting that person's infected blood into your bloodstream.

3) You can get HIV by getting a blood transfusion from someone who is infected.

A blood transfusion is when you get blood or blood components given (donated) by someone else. You might get a blood transfusion in the hospital if you've been in an accident and have lost a lot of blood or if you're having an operation or if you have hemophilia, a rare inherited disease that makes people bleed easily.

Before 1985, a number of people who got blood transfusions got infected with HIV because they were given donated blood that was infected with the virus. In 1985, a screening test was developed to detect HIV antibodies in donated blood. Since then, **all blood that is donated for blood transfusions is tested for HIV.**

That means that the risk of being infected with

22

HIV from transfusions has been very low since 1985. Nevertheless, it is possible—although not likely—for someone to get the virus from a contaminated blood transfusion or organ transplant. This could happen if the person who donated the blood was infected with the virus so recently that he or she hasn't yet tested positive for it, so the infected blood isn't rejected for donation (see below). Medical authorities recommend that anyone who is planning surgery store some of his or her own blood ahead of time, so that person can be sure of a safe transfusion. **But the risk of getting HIV from a blood transfusion today is very small.** You're about forty times more likely to die in a car crash on the highway than you are to get HIV from a blood transfusion.

You can't get HIV from *donating* blood, since brand-new needles and syringes are used for each donation and then they are immediately destroyed so no one can use them again.

4) A pregnant woman with HIV can pass the virus to her child before or after birth.
A fetus (unborn baby) gets its nourishment from its mother through the placenta and the umbilical cord, the group of blood vessels that attach the baby to the mother at the baby's navel (belly button). If a pregnant woman has HIV in her blood, it is possible that she can pass it along to her fetus during the pregnancy or during the actual birth of the baby. The baby

after being diagnosed with AIDS.

23

can be born with HIV. Although less common, it is also possible that an infected mother could give the virus to her child if she breast-feeds the baby, because HIV also appears in breast milk.

Some of the babies that are born with HIV are born to mothers who use drugs. That means their babies are born not only infected with HIV but also addicted to the drug their mother was taking. These infants start life off with two strikes against them—drug addiction and HIV infection.

In the United States, 25 percent to 30 percent of all babies that are born to HIV-infected mothers will actually be infected with the virus. These infected infants and children will eventually develop AIDS. The others initially test positive because antibodies from the mother cross the placenta into the fetus, making the HIV antibody test positive. However, unless the virus has also infected the fetus or infant, the antibodies from the mother will disappear within eighteen months and the HIV antibody test will no longer be positive. These infants are not infected and can grow and develop normally.

am I at risk for HIV?

HIV and AIDS can threaten anyone, anywhere; it all depends on what you do.

Scientists don't know for sure how many people have HIV, because many people who are infected don't know they have it. The Centers for Disease Control and Prevention estimates there are about 1 million people in the United States with HIV. The World Health Organization estimates that 19 to 20 million people around the world today have HIV. It also estimates that by the year 2000, 30 to 40 million men, women, and children all over the world will be infected with HIV, with about 36 million of those in developing countries. Scientists do have a better idea of how many people in the United States have AIDS because most of those cases do get reported.

There are people with AIDS in every state: men, women, and children of every race and color and of every age—from newborn babies to people over the age of 65. AIDS is in every community and will keep spreading unless we pay attention and stop it.

Some people think that getting HIV is something that happens only to other people. They are wrong. I want to clear up a number of widespread myths:

"HIV happens only to gays or bisexuals."

WRONG. Outside of the United States, especially in developing countries, most people with AIDS are heterosexual—in fact, about 75 percent of the people with AIDS throughout the world are heterosexual. And 90 percent of new adult infections worldwide involve heterosexuals. While it's currently true that at this time in the United States, three out of every five people with AIDS are gay or bisexual men, the number of heterosexual men and women with AIDS in this country is rising. And if we look only at AIDS cases, we are looking at the epidemic as long as ten years ago, because that's how long, on average, it takes to go from HIV infection to AIDS. In the United States, HIV is now spreading more quickly among heterosexual men and women than among homosexuals or bisexuals—probably because many heterosexuals don't believe they can get infected and don't protect themselves! In New York City, over half of the people with AIDS are heterosexual.

Your sexual orientation has nothing to do with your risk of getting HIV. Being gay or bisexual doesn't cause AIDS. Many people wrongly believe that, because AIDS was first recognized in America in gay and bisexual men.

But those men didn't get HIV because they were gay or bisexual; they got it because they transmitted the virus through risky behavior such as unprotected sex and sharing needles. When heterosexuals engage in the same risky behavior, they put themselves at the same risk of getting HIV as homosexuals.

For example, some heterosexual men have anal sex with women—for birth control, to protect the woman's virginity, out of curiosity, or simply because they like the way it feels. Some men have anal sex with men but don't consider themselves homosexual or bisexual, because they generally feel themselves most strongly attracted sexually to women. The point is, unprotected anal sex is very risky behavior, no mat-

if you get infected with HIV, it can take six months

ter who does it. And men and women have unprotected vaginal sex, because they're using other birth control methods or they don't want to use condoms for whatever reason. That's risky behavior, too.

"I'm not a druggie, so I don't have to worry, right?"

WRONG. Many people get HIV because they have unprotected sex with people who got HIV from sharing needles. And those people can give the virus to other people through unprotected sex.

"I'm too young to get AIDS."

WRONG. Teenagers get AIDS, too. **One out of every five people with AIDS today probably was infected when he or she was a teenager.** Remember that the symptoms of infection may take many years to appear. In New York City alone, there are an estimated 10,000 to 40,000 adolescents infected with HIV *who do not know they have the virus.*

Most teenagers don't see other teenagers around them dying of AIDS. But it happens.

"I'm Hispanic. I thought only white people get HIV."

WRONG. Most of the people who were initially diagnosed with AIDS in the United States were gay white

for the virus to show up in an HIV antibody test.

men. But more and more black, Hispanic, Asian, and Native American people—gay and straight—are getting AIDS and the rate of infection in the black community is increasing at a frightening rate. About 40 percent of people with AIDS are black. About 19 percent of people with AIDS are Hispanic. Some people from Asia and the Pacific Islands and Native Americans also have AIDS. Anybody can get HIV. No one is immune.

"I'm a woman. Am I really at risk for getting HIV?"

YES. Nearly 15 percent of the people with AIDS in the United States are female. And remember, that's women who were infected an average of ten years ago. Women are now probably closer to 20 percent of those who are HIV-infected! In New York City, AIDS is the number-one killer of young adult women. The high rate of HIV infection among women corresponds directly to the high rate of HIV infection among babies in New York City.

"I'm a lesbian, so I don't have to worry about getting HIV, do I?"

WRONG. There are many lesbians in the United States with HIV. Lesbians are most at risk of HIV infection through shared needles and works. Women who have sex with women should also remember that

HIV can be transmitted through unprotected oral sex and the sharing of sex toys that have been used in the vagina or rectum of an infected woman.

"I don't have to worry about HIV. I don't do high-risk sex or shoot drugs."
WRONG. AIDS is also killing a lot of people who never had any high-risk sex or shared any needles with persons infected with HIV:

▶ Even though both partners in a relationship might be monogamous, one partner might unknowingly have gotten HIV years before entering the present relationship. Or one of the partners could step out of the relationship, get the virus, and pass it to the other, faithful partner.

▶ *You* don't have to use drugs or share needles to get HIV; if your sexual partner did or does, you could become infected from unprotected sex with your partner.

▶ You could be among the handful of men, women, and children who got HIV from blood transfusions that screened negative for HIV, meaning the blood was supposedly free of HIV but was really contaminated.

▶ Babies born to mothers infected with the virus could get it, too, before or during birth, or possibly from infected breast milk.

Remember: You don't get HIV because of who you are; you get it because of what you do.

If your gut started flipping while you were reading this but your head still says, "This could never possibly happen to me," you are still in denial. When I first announced I had HIV, people who didn't know me tried to put a label on me—gay, bisexual—anything so they wouldn't have to admit that a heterosexual man had gotten the virus. Maybe that brought it too close to home for them. That was just another type of denial. If you think HIV could never happen to you, you're dead wrong.

You don't catch HIV the way you catch a cold or the flu.
You don't get HIV from casual contact.
HIV is different from other viruses you hear about. You don't "catch" it the same way you catch a cold, the flu, or chicken pox. In fact, you don't catch this virus unless you've been doing the kind of risky stuff we already talked about. One study was done on 600 families—2,400 people—in which one person in each family was HIV-infected. Even though they shared towels, toilets, cooking utensils, dishes, knives, forks, spoons, razors—and 7 percent of them even shared *toothbrushes*—not one family member got HIV from casual contact with the infected person.

Can I get HIV from kissing?

As far as we know, no one has ever gotten HIV from casual "dry" kissing.

Theoretically, you could get HIV from French-kissing (open-mouth, "deep," or "tongue"-kissing) someone who is infected if both of you have open sores or cuts on your lips or inside your mouth or if your gums are bleeding (for example, after brushing or flossing). However, as far as scientists know, no one has ever gotten HIV from French-kissing.

Since you don't get HIV from saliva, that means you don't get HIV from sharing a can of soda or a glass of water with someone who has HIV. And you don't get it from sharing cups, plates, or eating utensils. Remember:

▶ You don't get HIV from eating food that has been prepared or served by someone with HIV.
▶ You don't get HIV from sharing a cigarette, cigar, or pipe with someone who has HIV—but stop smoking anyway!
▶ You don't get HIV from a drinking fountain.
▶ You don't get HIV from someone spitting on you.

Can I get HIV from hugging?

No. HIV isn't transmitted through casual physical contact, and that includes not only hugging but holding hands, shaking hands, and slow-dancing, or more. You don't get HIV from massaging, tickling, or otherwise touching someone else's healthy skin. (See Chapter 3, "How to Have Safer Sex.") Your skin protects you wonderfully from HIV and other infections. It's especially important to remember that if you meet someone with HIV. Cutting off physical contact only makes people with HIV feel even more isolated and alone. Hugging someone with HIV is sometimes the best medicine for both of you.

Can I get HIV from sweat, tears, or mucus?
No. Even though there are sometimes tiny amounts of HIV in tears, you don't get HIV from someone else's sweat, tears, coughs, or sneezes or from sharing a used handkerchief.

Can I get HIV from an infected person's urine (pee) or stool (bowel movement, feces)?
No one has ever gotten HIV from an infected person's urine or stool, although it's theoretically possible if there's visible blood. However, since you can get other diseases such as parasites (worms) and hepatitis (infection of the liver) from handling someone else's stool, you should be careful to avoid coming into contact with it. If you have to clean up someone's urine or stool, wear vinyl or rubber gloves and be sure to wash your hands thoroughly with soap and water as soon as you finish—and be especially careful not to put your dirty fingers near your mouth or eyes.

a pregnant woman infected with HIV can

Can I get HIV from an infected person's cut or nosebleed?

Theoretically, it's possible. Also, other diseases like hepatitis can be passed this way, so if you have to clean up after someone's cut or nosebleed, use proper first-aid procedures. Wear vinyl or rubber gloves, and be sure to wash your hands thoroughly with soap and water as soon as you finish.

Can I get HIV from a health-care worker (doctor, nurse, hospital orderly, dentist, etc.)?

Many people worry that you can get HIV from a health-care worker because these people often work with people with AIDS and come into contact with their blood. **Even if you were treated by a health-care worker infected with HIV, the chances of that person infecting you are remote.**

The only such case ever recorded in medical history was the case of a Florida dentist who died of AIDS after passing it along to five of his patients. Scientists still aren't sure how the infected dentist could have passed along HIV. Today all dentists should wear vinyl or latex gloves and sterilize their equipment before performing any dental work—for your protection and theirs.

The fact is, health-care workers face a greater risk of getting HIV from infected patients than you do of getting HIV from an infected health-care worker. Health-care workers take special precautions to pro-

pass the virus to her unborn child.

tect themselves and all their patients. These precautions also help protect uninfected patients from getting HIV from a health-care worker who is infected. Remember: You put your health more at risk by not getting the medical or dental attention you need than by staying away from health-care workers because of the unnecessary fear of getting HIV.

Can I get HIV from giving blood?

No! This is one of the most common myths about how you can get HIV. **You can't get HIV from giving blood.** When you donate blood, health-care workers use a brand-new needle to take the blood out of your arm, and they destroy that needle as soon as you've finished donating blood, so that it can't be reused. One of the saddest things about the HIV epidemic is that America's blood supply is very low because some people are afraid to give blood. They don't understand that it's impossible to get HIV this way.

Can I get HIV from a mosquito?

No. Even though there are some diseases, such as malaria, that can be spread by mosquitoes, you can't get HIV from a mosquito. And you can't get HIV from any other biting or stinging insects such as flies, fleas, bedbugs, or lice.

Can I get HIV from pets or any other animal?
No, you can't catch HIV from any animal. Remember, HIV stands for *human* immunodeficiency virus. Animals can't get HIV, and you can't catch any AIDS-like illness from any animal. A certain species of African monkey can have a condition similar to AIDS but cannot give it to humans.

Can I get HIV from a toilet seat?
No. You don't get HIV from a toilet seat, telephone, doorknob, typewriter or computer keyboard, swimming pool, Jacuzzi, steam room, sauna, shower, bathtub, bath towels, clothing, a locker room floor, or pens or pencils. There is some small theoretical risk if there is visible blood in any of these places.

Can I get HIV from sharing makeup with someone who's infected?
No. You don't get HIV from sharing any makeup—including lipstick—with someone who has HIV. However, you can get other infections from sharing makeup.

If someone with HIV bites, scratches, cuts, or spits on me, can I get HIV?
Skin is a good defense against HIV. Unless blood from an opening in the skin of an infected person comes into contact with an opening in your skin, HIV doesn't get transmitted.

do I need to get an HIV antibody test?

As you read this book, you might start to remember things you've done that could have infected you with HIV. Don't panic. You may want to talk to someone you can trust, like your parents, a guidance counselor, a school nurse, a teacher, a doctor, and so on. If you're worried, your counselor may suggest you get tested. Think about whether testing is right for you. It's a serious decision, and it is yours to make. Make sure you're ready to hear the results. If you are infected, who will you tell about your results, and where can you get medical help and support? Be sure you get tested by someone who will give you counseling and information *before* and *after* the test. Think about why you want the test. Is it so you can feel safe? No matter what your test results, you still need to practice safer sex. And be sure to protect yourself and your sexual partners whether or not you get tested. You don't need to know if you are HIV-positive or HIV-negative to be safe.

I've already explained that when the virus enters your body, your immune system tries to fight it off. It does this by making something called **HIV antibodies,** which actually track down and attach themselves to the virus particles, as do certain white blood cells. It can take a few months after you've been infected for your body to make enough HIV antibodies to show up in a test—usually three months, but in rare cases it can take up to six months or longer. When you take an "AIDS test," you are really being tested to see if your body has begun to produce HIV antibodies, which is why the test is properly called the **HIV antibody test.** The test tells you if your body has begun making antibodies to the virus. If your body has begun making HIV antibodies, you've been infected with HIV.

How does the HIV antibody test work?

When you take the HIV antibody test, a health-care worker takes a small sample of blood from your arm. You can't get HIV from this test, because health-care workers use a brand-new needle for each blood sample and the needle is destroyed immediately afterward. It takes only a minute or so to take the blood for the test, and then the blood goes to a laboratory. It may take up to two or three weeks before you get the test results, depending on where you get tested.

You don't have to know all the details of the test, but sometimes you might hear it called the ELISA test, which stands for enzyme-linked immunoabsorbent assay. If two or more tests come out positive, health-care workers should do another test, called a Western Blot test, on the same blood sample to confirm the results. If the Western Blot test is positive, it means you have been infected with the virus and you have developed antibodies. This is what is known as "testing positive," "being seropositive," or "being HIV-positive."

What if they make a mistake on the test?

Although you may get a "false positive" test with the ELISA (meaning the test says you have HIV and you really don't), it is very unlikely that you would have a false positive test with the Western Blot.

You could also get what's called a "false negative" HIV antibody test. This means that the test says you don't have HIV infection when you really do. Since it may take up to six months for your body to build up enough HIV antibodies to be detectable, if you get tested too soon after you've been infected, you might get a false negative result. In addition, the laboratory performing the test could make a mistake. That's why you should consider getting tested more than once if you've engaged in risky behavior that might have infected you with HIV or you've had unprotected sex with someone who engaged in risky behavior. You can't have unprotected sex Saturday night and get tested Monday morning. The HIV antibodies can't show up by then. **To have confidence in the test results, you need to wait three to six months after your last risky behavior before you get tested. You'll have to forgo sex or have safer sex the entire time before you test.**

If you test negative for HIV antibodies, don't think, "Hey, I did whatever I wanted and I didn't get the virus, so I can keep right on doing it." Nobody is immune to HIV. You might not be so lucky the next time.

38

You may wonder, If your body makes antibodies to HIV, why don't those antibodies kill the virus and keep you from getting AIDS? HIV is a very unusual virus, and for some reason that we still don't understand, antibodies first keep the virus in check, but eventually the virus takes over.

Can I get tested without anyone else knowing about it?

It depends where you live. If you decide you want to get tested, I strongly recommend **anonymous testing.** With this kind of testing, your name is not recorded or revealed to anybody else. The best way to find anonymous testing is to call your local source for AIDS information (check the listings at the back of this book) or the CDC National HIV and AIDS Hotline (the toll-free number is 1 (800) 342-AIDS). (Spanish-speaking persons can call La Linea Nacional de SIDA—the toll-free number is 1 (800) 344-SIDA. Hearing-impaired persons can call the toll-free number TDD 1 (800) 243-7889.) You can also look in the phone book for your city's Public Health Department or Department of Public Health or City Department of Health. The test is usually free, and no one else has to know about it. In some parts of the country, however, anonymous testing isn't available, or you may find that if you are under 18 you can't get an HIV antibody test without your parents' permission. If that's the case for you and you don't want to have to

just once with someone who has the virus.

go to your parents for permission, call an AIDS hotline and see what your other options are. If you live in a small town or see a family doctor, it's sometimes harder to keep it a secret. Again, call an AIDS hotline and find out what you can do.

If you are tested anonymously, the clinic or laboratory gives you an appointment for the blood test and a number. When you give your blood sample, they put your number on the tube to be tested. Nobody ever asks you for your name. They'll tell you when to come back to get the results (usually after two or three weeks). The counselor looks up your number on a list to get the test results, and no one knows that the number is connected with your name. You should be offered counseling before and after the test. If you lose or forget your code number, you must start all over again with a new blood sample.

Another option is **confidential testing.** That means that your doctor is usually the only person who knows your HIV test result, which becomes part of your medical record. The only way that anyone else could find out about your test results is if you sign a medical release, for example, when you change doctors and your second doctor asks your permission to obtain your first doctor's records. Another way would be if a hospital requested your record if you had an accident or an illness. Still another way would be if an insurance company needed your record if you were trying to get an insurance policy. It was by having an HIV antibody test to get an insurance policy that I learned I was HIV-positive. I'm thankful I learned I was infected as soon as I did, because I was able to take action to prevent my wife and child from being infected and I could start preventive health care.

If you do decide to be tested, practically every testing site has a counselor who will try to talk to you about what the test means, what it means to be HIV-positive, what all the illnesses associated with AIDS are, how to get treatment and help, and how to avoid HIV. That person can answer your questions, ease a lot of your anxieties, and put to rest a lot of your doubts.

Why not test everybody for HIV?

That would be tremendously expensive. Everybody in the country would have to be tested every few months. Most public-health experts feel it would not be worth the cost. It makes better sense to spend money on education about AIDS so people can learn how to avoid the virus.

Can someone ever make me take the HIV antibody test?

Yes. You must take a blood test for HIV before you apply for certain government jobs, such as the uniformed services (Army, Navy, Air Force, etc.), the Peace Corps, the Job Corps, and the foreign service. You will be rejected for most of these jobs if you test positive. You'll also have to take the HIV antibody test if you're sent to prison. The Immigration and Naturalization Service (INS) usually allows someone who wants to visit the United States as a tourist to come in without taking the test. However, the United States keeps people out if they are HIV-positive and intend to live here for some length of time or permanently. Most other countries do not have such rules.

Every time you donate blood, that blood is tested for HIV. If it is positive, the blood bank will be in touch with you and counsel you. **This is completely confidential.** So be generous and give blood for transfusions. But if you have engaged in risky behavior, **don't** donate blood as a way of being tested for HIV. If you are early in the antibody development period, your blood could infect someone else. Go to an anonymous counseling and testing center instead.

is there a vaccine to prevent HIV/AIDS?

Not yet. You may have heard that scientists are trying to develop a vaccine against HIV. A vaccine is a substance that helps your immune system protect you from a specific disease. When you were a young child, for example, you were almost certainly vaccinated against polio, whooping cough, and measles, along with other illnesses, so that you wouldn't catch these illnesses from others. But there is no vaccine to pre-

42

vent HIV yet, and there may not be one before the end of this century.

It's best not to pin your hopes on a scientific breakthrough. Instead, you should learn how to protect yourself against HIV in the first place. Once you get HIV, you don't get a second chance to be more careful the next time around.

*t*here is no cure yet for AIDS

1. To the best of our knowledge, once you catch HIV through unprotected sex or sharing works when you shoot drugs, you will always have the virus. And you will always be able to infect other people, unless you practice prevention.

2. You can *get* the infection without knowing it. You can *spread* the infection without knowing it. You can have HIV and look and feel just as well as you ever did for months or even years.

3. People don't die of AIDS—they die of diseases that AIDS lets

—no matter what you're shooting.

invade their body, such as pneumonia, cancer, tuberculosis, and so on, that their immune systems cannot control.

4. There is a blood test that can tell you if you have HIV. The test measures the HIV antibodies you have in your body. If you have been infected, it takes time—three to six months or more—for your body to make enough of these antibodies to make the HIV antibody test positive.

5. Treatments for HIV infection are available. They do the most good when you start taking them early.

what should I do if I test positive for HIV?

Don't despair, and don't panic. Ask your doctor a lot of questions. You'll learn you can keep on living if you treat yourself properly. Once I found that out, I had a great attitude. I didn't panic. Please see Chapter 6 for more information about living with HIV.

"I have HIV."

a ntigone, *who was 23 when she was interviewed, relates "what they didn't tell me in high school."*

Hello, my name is Antigone, which is my real name. I was born during the "summer of love" and was given a real name that actually would make a great pseudonym. Last year I found out that I am HIV-positive. At the time, I was 22 years old and I had a year and a half of sobriety. Since that day, I have gone through many changes. I have worked through my initial shock at learning that I was infected through heterosexual sex when I was a teenager.

The first three months after my diagnosis were very difficult. I had a hard time doing basic things like riding the bus and going to school. At school I was around people my age who would talk about their lives and futures in an open-ended way. I had difficulty relating at first. Most young people don't sit around coffee shops talking about death and sickness. I felt so different. I began to get resentful and felt, "Why did this happen to me?" Everything I read about HIV made it seem so hard for women, especially young women, to get infected through heterosexual sex.

As I struggled with these feelings and

thoughts, I joined the only support group for HIV-positive young people under the age of 25. Just walking into a room full of other young people who were dealing with this disease filled me with a wonderful feeling of hope. Going to the group gave me the courage to do many of the things that I have done since that awful week a year ago.

During those first three months, I attempted to work and go to school but ended up staying home a lot and playing Nintendo. I needed something more. I quit my old job and became a peer educator.

This was when my anger started to surface— anger that my high school never said anything to me about my risk for HIV infection, anger at the service providers who treated me for other sexually transmitted diseases but never told me that I should practice safer sex. And anger at doctors who told me that they could tell by looking at me that I was HIV-negative. Many of these people gave me birth control pills and washed their hands of me.

When I decided that I wanted to become a peer educator, I was lucky to get the opportunity to do so. I had no prior experience, just a need to be doing something. My co-workers treated me as an equal, and they respected my feelings about not disclosing during presentations. They let me be Antigone the peer educator, not Antigone who is HIV-positive. This was what I badly needed. When I found out I was HIV-positive, I began to lose sight of myself. They helped put me back on track.

Soon I felt ready to share my experience with other young people. The Wedge Program [a San Francisco Bay Area–based program for teens] gave me the opportunity and strength to do it. As a speaker with the Wedge, I have gone back to my old high school and shared my story. What an empowering experience!

I have had a very hard time finding a peer group of other HIV-positive young women. So many times I have felt like an anomaly: Either I am the only woman or I am the youngest person with HIV. But I feel lucky that caring and supportive people have been put in my life because of this disease. Though my life has changed drastically in the past year, I have found new goals and new hopes. So far these feelings have not abandoned me, and I pray they never will. ■

CHAPTER 2
how to be
sexually
responsible

understanding your sexual feelings

Sexual desire is perfectly natural, and sexual fulfillment is a very important part of most people's lives. The challenge we all face is to learn how to express our sexuality in ways that respect others as well as ourselves. And now, in the age of AIDS, the challenge is even greater, for we have to learn how to express our sexuality and gratify our desires in ways that don't risk the health of others or ourselves.

Sexual responsibility means more than deciding when to have sex—and here I'm talking about sexual intercourse—or with whom. It means more than taking steps to avoid HIV or other STDs or an unwanted pregnancy. It means taking charge of your body and your choices, sorting out your feelings and values, and learning to live by them.

That's easy to say and hard to do, especially when everyone on TV and in the movies seems to be hopping into bed with everyone else without giving it a moment's thought.

having sexual feelings doesn't mean you have to act on them.

Some people are easily able to handle their sexual feelings, while others are frightened by them. Some people become sexually active earlier than others. I think the best thing you can do if you're a teenager is postpone sexual activity with another person for as long as possible. That way, you not only have a better chance of finding a lasting, loving relationship, but you won't have to worry about getting pregnant or catching an STD. Some people never have sex until they're married.

Maybe you've spent time with people who are always bragging about who they slept with. You know if you told them you were a virgin, they'd look down on you. If these are the kind of friends you've got, maybe they aren't your friends. Mature people who are sexually active don't make fun of those who don't have sex. And lots of people who say they're sexually active with other people aren't. Many people feel the way you do. Go find them and hang out with them.

A lot of the teenagers I've talked to who are sexually active worry because of HIV and other STDs and pregnancy, and they actually think the kids who don't have sex are making safer decisions. If you don't want to have sex with another person, you don't owe anybody else a reason—it's your choice.

> **did you know that 1 million teenage girls get pregnant every year?**
> **did you know that 44 percent of all adolescent girls get pregnant at least once as teenagers?**

It's okay to have sexual thoughts and feelings—fantasies are normal. But you shouldn't feel you have to act on them until you're good and ready. You're the one who decides when it's time to be sexually active (unless you're the survivor of rape, incest, or sexual abuse), and you should base that decision on your own values and beliefs. Most people rely on the values they've learned from their family, community, or religion.

If you have been sexually abused or raped right to choice was taken away from you. Please derstand that what happened is not your fault, and it doesn't have anything to do with your worth as a person. Please try to get help: Call your local rape-crisis hotline and find someone you can talk to who understands what you're going through and can advise you.

Some people have sex because they're curious. Some have sex because they want to experiment. Other people think it's cool to be able to tell a friend how many sexual partners they have had. Some people feel pressured into having sex by others who tell them they're not a real man or a real woman unless they "do it." Some people want to know if they can make a baby. Some people think having a baby is like having a wonderful doll that you can put on the shelf when you're tired of playing with it and you want to do something else. And some people think they are in love.

You can have sex in a few minutes, but it takes a long time to build trust in a friendship. Having sex with somebody early in a relationship does not prove to either partner that this is love. And having sex because you want to be loved and cherished doesn't guarantee that your partner will love you back—he or she may not even *like* you back! Many people say that sex is most wonderful when it is part of a very special relationship that has taken a long time to build, when it is part of the mutual caring and security of a lasting commitment.

I'm not here to tell you that there's only one "right" reason to have sex. But before you have sex with someone, ask yourself why you want to. How do you feel about this person? Is he or she worthy of your intimacy and respect? Are you under any pressure from this person or from others to have sex? Are you trying to prove you're a real man or a real woman? How will having sex change your relationship with this person? If you never saw this person again after you had sex, how would you feel about it? Respect the people you're with. Respect yourself the most.

how does having sex fit into your dreams?

What roles do you want sex, love, and affection to play in your life? Here's one way to think about how the sex you have now can affect what you want out of life in the future:

First, think about something you're looking forward to in the future. It could be a wonderful relationship, a great place to live, a really interesting career, raising a family, or all these things plus a great sex life into the bargain.

Now, think about how having HIV or another STD or an unwanted pregnancy would affect your dreams. If you had HIV, you might be too sick to get what you want, or you might suffer discrimination that would keep you from fulfilling your dream, or you could die long before you got your dream. Some

52

STDs can make you sterile, so you could neve[r have] children of your own. Some STDs can make it [more] likely that you'll get cancer. How would you deal with an unwanted pregnancy, and how would it stand in the way of your dreams? How would you feel if your baby was born with HIV?

different people have different sexual orientations. They are all normal.

Another part of sexual responsibility is coming to terms with the way you are. There are three different sexual orientations: heterosexuality (sexual attraction to someone of the opposite sex, sometimes called "being straight"), homosexuality (sexual attraction to someone of the same sex, sometimes called "being gay" or "being lesbian"), and bisexuality (sexual attraction to people of both sexes, sometimes called "being bi").

No one knows why one person has a particular sexual orientation. *It is quite usual for young people growing up to have a wide variety of sexual feelings about and attractions to people of the same and opposite sex.* Some people recognize their own sexual orientation very young, while others may not be sure of it until they're in their teens or older. That's okay. It may take you some time to become comfortable with your sexual orientation. Remember: Your sexual orientation isn't something you choose; it's something you are.

in the United States have HIV.

f you're considering becoming sexually active, you should ask yourself the following questions:

▶ Am I prepared to practice safer sex each and every time I have sex?

▶ Am I prepared to use contraception each and every time I have man-woman sex?

▶ Am I prepared to deal with the consequences if I or a partner becomes infected with HIV or another STD or becomes pregnant?

▶ Am I prepared to say no when I think it's not right for me?

If you say yes to these questions while you're still a teenager, I have to ask, "Are you sure?" If you can still honestly answer yes to all these questions, maybe you're starting to understand what sexual responsibility is all about. If you're not prepared to act in ways that are sexually responsible, then you're putting yourself and your partners at risk. A lot of people want sex, but they don't want to have to deal with the responsibility that comes along with it—and in the age of AIDS, that's a **big** responsibility. One benefit of postponing sex is that you won't have to worry about HIV, other STDs, and pregnancy. The "safest sex," of course, is no sex. I think abstinence—not having sex—is a very responsible and difficult decision. If you decide to put off having sex, that's great. If you decide to

have sex, make a conscious decision to be resp   ·.
about it.

**If you don't know what you're do-
ing about sex . . . don't do it. Wait.**

if you can wait, wait

I remember what it's like to hear that when you're a
teenager. You're going to be curious about sex—it's all
over TV, videos, movies—and you might feel some
peer pressure about it. But if I had known what I do
now when I was younger, I would have postponed sex
as long as I could and I would have tried to have it the
first time with somebody that I knew I wanted to
spend the rest of my life with. I certainly want **my**
children to postpone sex. Now, the rest of my life may
be a lot shorter than I thought it was going to be, and
I may not be around to see my sons, Andre and
Earvin III, or my daughter, Elisa, grow up, and of
course I may not have the long life I want with
Cookie.

If you've got younger brothers and sisters, get
the message to them. Tell them there'll be plenty of
time for sex later on. Give them the facts so that they
know that choosing to have sex is a big decision, both
emotionally and for health reasons. But just as important, tell them to really think about what they want sex
to mean to them, and tell them you understand what
they're going through. Sometimes brothers and sisters
can say things that parents can't.

Not having vaginal, anal, or oral sex doesn't mean

at you can't be friendly with people, that you can't be close or loving with people, that you can't even touch or kiss people. You can show your love and affection to others, you can share the joys of each other's bodies, you can be really close to each other— and you don't need to have intercourse to do it. I'll talk more about this in the next chapter.

If you are already sexually active, I know you're probably not going to stop. But you do have that choice; it's something to consider. However, I realize that returning to abstinence isn't always realistic. But be smart enough to be careful. You've got to practice responsible, safer sex to protect yourself and your partner.

Every time you have unprotected sex with someone, it's as if you're also having sex with everyone else that person has had sex with. And since in some cases it can take ten years or more from the time someone is infected with HIV until he or she feels or looks sick, you have to be concerned about anybody your partner has had sex with in the last ten years. When someone has sex with you, he or she is having sex with everyone that *you* ever had sex with any time in your life.

Here's an example: Joe is a bartender. He has HIV (though he doesn't know it), but looks great and feels well.

Joe has unprotected sex with a lot of people, and he spreads the virus to Tricia and George.

Tricia has unprotected sex with Harry and gives

infected with HIV by the year 2000.

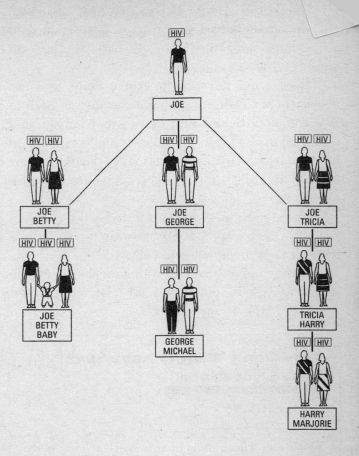

Here's how one person with HIV can unknowingly spread the virus to many others through unprotected sex.

nim the virus. Harry has unprotected sex with Marjorie and gives her the virus.

George has unprotected sex with Michael and gives him the virus.

Joe decides he wants to marry Betty, who has never had sex with anyone until she met and fell in love with Joe. Before long Betty gets pregnant, and when the doctors test her blood as she gets ready to have the baby, they find she has HIV. When her baby is born, the baby has HIV and continues to test positive for it.

In the meantime, Joe gets tested and realizes he has HIV. Joe has spread HIV to seven people—three men, three women, and one baby.

Having unprotected sex with a number of people is playing Russian roulette—it just takes one time for you to get HIV or another STD.

"You Don't Want to Have Sex? You're Not Alone."

by Kyeeniah Nix

note: *The names in this section have been changed.*

"Because the majority is out there having sex, it's like being born without eyes and a mouth if you haven't done it. It's like a trend, because everybody is doing it," says Carl, 19.

But who says everybody is having sex?

Believe it or not, there are thousands of teens in New York City who are abstaining (not having sex).

Unfortunately, these teens often hear name-calling and sarcasm.

"What's the matter, are you gay?" says one girl.

"Yo, man, you better get with it!" says one guy to a friend.

"What's the matter, baby, you think your vagina is too good for me?" says another guy to a girl.

Comments like these are used to put teens under pressure to have sex. Therefore, many are afraid to open up their feelings, to admit that they are virgins or that they are abstaining from sex.

"They don't want nobody to think they're a nerd, it's as simple as that," says John, 18, of Brooklyn. "They are afraid of how people would react."

John is one of the few teens who admit that they choose not to have sex.

"If I'm going to make love to the girl, I want her to enjoy it. I wouldn't have the guts to do that unless I was married. I don't want to force myself," he says.

Others who are abstinent mention how they

involve heterosexuals.

think a relationship should be *before* having sex. They mention what trust is to them and what love means to them.

"I'm looking for a relationship that is realistic, and we wouldn't have to prove anything to anyone but ourselves," says Alex, 17.

"I'm looking for someone who is honest and loyal, and could stand a long-lasting relationship that won't break easily," says Angel, 17.

"Sharing feelings is a two-way street. Both have to have love for each other . . . it takes time! How can I say I love him if we only knew each other for two weeks?" asks Jasmine, 17.

"Love is being a part of a person," says Angel, "feeling what that person is feeling and going through the pain with the person and being there afterward, no matter how high the waves are."

Alex has made up his mind to wait for that right person to enter his life, even though he feels it's going to take some time.

"It's better for me. When the waiting is over, it will be worth it," he says.

AIDS is going around, and this may be another reason why teens may not want to have sex.

"Everybody is scared of this disease. It kills!" says Jasmine. "Nobody really wants to get AIDS. I'm scared, and I'm not doing anything . . ."

Alexandra, 17, is not abstaining from sex, but she still feels that it is fine to abstain.

"I don't think people who don't have sex are strange. I think they are strong, and I admire them. People who make fun of them are scared of not being accepted and are insecure," she says.

How important is love in a sexual relationship? Are some people really putting it first?

"For me, love comes first," says Alexandra. "When I love someone, it's not sex, it's making love. It's sharing and becoming as close as we possibly can. When we make love, we incorporate mind, body, and soul. Unfortunately, many couples confuse love with lust," she says.

"I know that for a fact many people use that word [love] as a front, to get what they want, as if they were majoring in a Monopoly game. For me, that word is sacred. Throwing that word around, you're only making a fool of yourself," says Carl.

As a person who isn't abstinent, he still believes that there is nothing wrong with teens who say no to sex.

"That is cherishable because it is your body. You have to be strong. There's more beauty in that than just sharing your body. If you don't know why you're loving, you're not loving," Carl says.

Most of the teens interviewed feel strongly

about getting to know all about a person before having sex. They don't want to rush anything, because it's hard to find someone you can really trust.

"Without trust you have nothing. A solid relationship doesn't happen overnight. It takes weeks, months, and sometimes years," says Alexandra.

If you have never had sex and plan to wait, don't feel you have to apologize for anything. You are all right, and you are doing things at your own pace. Everybody moves at a different pace—you can feel free to move at yours.

Having sex is a big responsibility, and when you do it, you want to do it right. It takes time! ∎

Some people who choose mutually faithful monogamy—meaning they have sex with only one person and that person has sex only with them—choose a single partner for life. Others engage in "serial monogamy," meaning they have only one sex partner at a time. Some of these serially monogamous relationships last only a few weeks or months. The point is, monogamy means different things to different people. **Being in a monogamous relationship doesn't mean you don't have to be concerned about safer sex.** You must be sexually responsible for each and every relationship you have.

62 ══════

I'm talking about sex with self-respect and with mutual respect.

If you're in a lifelong mutually faithful, monogamous relationship and neither of you shoots drugs, there will come a time when you can have unprotected sex with little risk of getting HIV—but you had better talk to a doctor or HIV counselor about that. In the meantime, use a latex condom from start to finish every time you have sex.

You and your partner should consider going to a doctor or clinic and taking the HIV antibody test to see if either of you has the virus. But remember: This is a serious decision, and you may want to talk to a counselor before you make it. Hopefully, neither of you will have a positive test, but you can't be sure that you don't have HIV, because you might have been infected too recently for your body to have made the antibodies against HIV that would make the test positive. Therefore, the doctor or clinic will recommend that you keep using condoms for a certain time—at least six months and maybe longer—before you take the test again. If you both test negative that second time, the doctor or clinic will probably tell you it's okay to have unprotected sex with each other.

If you have a steady sexual partner and you're tempted to have sex with someone else, remember that you're risking not only your health but also the health of your partner. **If you are sexually active and understand what sex and re-**

sponsibility are all about, please be careful and practice safer sex.

Please notice: I said **"safer sex,"** not **"safe sex." In today's world, there is no such thing as absolutely "safe sex" when we're talking about intercourse.** Everything in life has risks attached. When you cross the street, you follow the traffic light and look both ways to reduce your risk. But you can't eliminate all risk and still cross the street: There is still a very, very small chance that you could be hit by a car. Safer sex works the same way: By using latex condoms properly, you can substantially reduce your risk of getting HIV, but you can't eliminate it entirely. That's why it's important to think about whether what a sexual relationship will give you outweighs the risk of having sex.

talking to your partner about sex and drugs

If you choose to have sex, make a promise to yourself to talk to your partner about sex and drugs **before** you decide to have sex with that person. You need to know more about the person you want to have sex with than where he or she works or goes to school or lives, what kind of music he or she likes, what other things you have in common—or even whether he or she loves you.

Maybe you can't picture yourself asking these kinds of questions in the heat of the moment. So don't wait until you're in bed to ask. Some people suggest you even make a date—maybe go out for lunch or coffee—just to talk about sex. You will probably discover right away that you're *both* scared to talk about sex and contraception and disease. It takes a lot of courage to talk to your partner about sex. If you're embarrassed or worried that you might insult your partner, think about this: If you feel strongly enough about someone else to want to have sex with him or her, you should be close enough to ask the questions that can protect your health. How your partner responds will tell you a lot about his or her values and character.

Being in love doesn't mean you don't have to deal with this. You've got to separate the issues of loving each other and the risk of HIV infection. **The two issues don't have anything to do with each other.** Good communication is part of every healthy sexual relationship. You can say, "It doesn't affect how much I love you, but there is this risk, and we have to talk about it."

This kind of frank talk gives you a chance to get to understand your partner's values and expectations. Reaching this level of intimacy can be difficult, but the reward is a closer relationship. This conversation doesn't have to be just about "Do we have sex or not?" or "Are we going to use a condom or not?" This is the time when you can ask each other, "What do you know about HIV and AIDS? What do you think about it? Well, if you're worried and I'm worried, what can we do? What are our options?"

If you still can't picture yourself starting this kind of conversation with your partner, see if you can get a good friend to do some role-playing with you, or ask a few friends how they talked to their partners.

I know this is asking a lot of you. Almost everyone has a hard time speaking frankly with others about sex. This is especially true when it comes to talking with someone you want to get involved with sexually. The embarrassment you may feel about speaking with another about such a sensitive subject is natural. But don't let it stop you. Even after two people have had sex, they may still find it hard to communicate honestly and openly with each other. But the silence that often surrounds sex needs to be broken if we are to have a fighting chance of ending the HIV and AIDS epidemic.

how can you tell if someone has HIV or another STD?

YOU CAN'T! No matter what he or she says, you can never really know for sure whether someone has HIV unless he or she has tested positive for the infection. There are several reasons for this: Your partner might not know he or she is infected; or he or she could be in denial, or might not be being completely honest with you. As far as other STDs are concerned, it's also true that you can never really know if a partner's been infected. A lot of people can have an STD and never know it, and they can easily pass it on to anybody they have unprotected sex with.

nearly 15 percent of all people with AIDS are female.

The most responsible thing to do is to act as though you yourself and anybody you want to have sex with could have HIV and to practice safer sex every time.

I know this is hard to accept. The best relationships—the relationships you probably want the most—are based on honesty and trust and love. And what I've just told you about practicing safer sex every time sounds as if I'm saying that you just can't trust anyone, no matter how much you love each other or how long you've known each other or how much honesty there is between the two of you. If you love someone and believe that person when he or she says he doesn't have HIV, it's hard to have to go ahead and practice safer sex anyway. But please understand me. I'm not saying all lovers are liars. I'm saying that, unfortunately, we now must all live in a world where HIV is this reality that everybody—even someone deeply in love—has to deal with. And the best way to show each other love is to take care of each other the best way you know how—and that means practicing safer sex.

So be smart and be responsible. If you choose not to have sex right now, you're making the safest choice. You're being your own person, and wonderful opportunities for the loving, caring relationship you want still lie ahead, untouched by past experience. If you choose to have sex, then please choose safer sex each and every time. The next chapter will tell you how.

"I have HIV."

david was a 21-year-old dancer with AIDS when this was written.

David Kamens is tall and thin, with sandy-brown hair and a quick smile. Like many 21-year-olds, David is out on his own, living with a friend in Washington, D.C. But David deals with more than rent, groceries, and laundry each month.

David has AIDS. A dancer with a bright future, David was afflicted with cytomegalovirus, a virus that strikes people with AIDS, just days before he was set to leave on tour with the Hungarian State School of Ballet in 1988. "I went from weighing 165 to 135 in three weeks," David recalls. "I had a high fever—104 degrees—and I was in bed for two months."

David, who is gay, believes he contracted HIV at 17 from having unprotected sex with a man he met at a bar. He admits that he was going through a wild period. "When you're a teenager, you experiment," David explains. "It's about being young—figuring out who you are and what you want. I was still dealing with my sexuality."

Although David knew about HIV and AIDS, he didn't really think he could get it. "I was only 17, and I felt like I was invulnerable," he says.

almost 40 percent of people with AIDS in the

"Plus, I was into cocaine and alcohol. When you're drinking and on drugs, nothing matters. You don't know what you're doing. When I was with someone, I didn't talk about AIDS. I didn't ask, and I trusted people I shouldn't have. For me, sex was tied to my sense of worth. I didn't think I could get AIDS."

But he did. Although he was sick in July of 1988, he didn't get positive proof until a few months later. When his test came back, he was devastated. "After I found out I was HIV-positive," David says, "I remember saying, 'This is it. I'm gone.'"

His attitude has changed, though. "I decided, hey, I'm only 18. I'm not going to let this thing get me down."

Despite his positive attitude, some days David feels down. He has sore throats a lot, and sometimes he aches all over. He battles a constant feeling of tiredness, and his hair is turning gray. He swallows a large amount of medication each day, not including the vitamins he takes. "I have to watch my health more carefully," he says. "I've been living with this for three years, and I plan to live with it for a long time."

David no longer dances, because he doesn't have the strength to put in the hours of grueling practice. Now he devotes himself to helping people understand AIDS. He is open about his condition; he has spoken at seminars at colleges and high schools across the country about living with AIDS.

"Maybe it would have made a difference if someone had told me that AIDS was a reality, that it could affect my life," says David. "I was ignorant, young enough so that I had never seen anyone with AIDS. Until you can put a face to AIDS, it isn't real." ∎

On February 28, 1992, as the original edition of this book was going to press, David Kamens died from complications of AIDS. "David lived his life to the fullest," said his parents, Nancy and Gerald Kamens. "He always said he wanted to dance till he dropped, and that's what he did." David believed strongly in AIDS education and awareness. His review of the manuscript of this book was a very important contribution. David was 21.

CHAPTER 3
how to have
safer sex

remember: You can't tell who has HIV by looking at anyone

You have the power to choose to be safe.

express yourself

As I've said, the safest choice is to postpone sex for now. That means enjoying a really close, intimate relationship, but not having vaginal, anal, or oral sex together.

We are all constantly bombarded by messages—especially from some TV shows and movies—that tell us that the only way you can have a satisfying sex life is if you have vaginal, anal, or oral sex. I disagree. You can still explore yourself sexually in ways that don't risk your health. You may be surprised at all the ways you can give and receive sexual pleasure that don't involve the risk of blood, semen, or vaginal fluids getting inside each other's bodies. Here's how some teenagers said they'd express themselves sexually without having vaginal, anal, or oral sex:

▶ Kissing
▶ Holding hands
▶ Hugging, cuddling, squeezing, and holding each other
▶ Talking, flirting, hanging out
▶ Dancing—slow-dancing, any kind of dancing
▶ Dressing up in sexy clothes
▶ Massaging each other

This could be just the beginning of the list for you. Just remember that you don't have to have intercourse to show how sexy you are or make yourself or your partner feel good or to express your love. Just because you don't have intercourse doesn't mean you're a prude. **You don't have to have sex to be sexy, and having sex doesn't**

72

make you sexy. Sexiness is a very individual thing. A lot of people say that sexy is what you are, not what you do.

You may already have discovered that some of the best moments in any relationship are the times the two of you just hung out with each other, spending hours just talking or listening to music.

how to have safer vaginal, anal, or oral sex

If you do decide that you want to have vaginal, anal, or oral sex with your partner, make the choice to have safer, protected sex *each and every time. That means using a latex condom (see below) every time you have sex.* Condoms offer the best available protection against HIV and other STDs besides abstinence. Don't try to figure out whether your partner is "risky" or "safe." You can't. If you have unprotected sex with *anyone,* you are at risk. Period.

But remember: No condom is guaranteed 100 percent effective in preventing HIV or other STDs. There are practically no guarantees in life. But don't let the small risk make you think, "Well, if I'm still at risk no matter what I do, why should I bother with safer sex?" You're still much, much better protected from STDs and unwanted pregnancy when you use a latex condom than when you don't.

Also remember: You can't think straight if you're on drugs or alcohol. That means you're more likely to take foolish chances—like having unprotected sex or sharing needles. You don't need drugs or alcohol to have a good time or good sex.

How do condoms work?

I'll spell it out step by step shortly, but here are the basics. A condom is a thin sheath that covers the tip and shaft of the penis. When a man wearing a condom ejaculates (comes), the semen fills up the tip of the condom. The condom works as a contraceptive (birth control device) by keeping the sperm in the semen away from the woman's egg so she won't get pregnant. Condoms can also help protect against HIV and other STDs. Condoms keep the wearer's penis from coming into contact with any blood or vaginal fluids from his partner's vagina, cervix, vulva, rectum, or mouth or with any cuts, sores, or warts in those places. Condoms keep the wearer's partner from coming into contact with semen, blood, or other discharges from the penis or with any cuts, warts, or sores on the head or shaft of the penis.

What kind of condom works best?

Use latex rubber condoms. Studies have shown that latex condoms can help protect against HIV and other STDs. Natural or "skin" condoms, which are made from sheep intestines, don't protect as well against HIV because the pores in the natural condoms are big enough for HIV to pass through.

Look for the word "latex" on the label before you buy.

Are lubricated condoms better?

All condoms need lubrication if they are going to be used for vaginal or anal sex. (Dry ones are best for oral sex.) But the kind of lubricant you use is very important, because using the wrong lube can make the condom break.

Use only water-based lubricants like K-Y Jelly or other lubricants made especially for sex. **Never** use lubricants containing oil, because they will make the condom break. Lubricants with oil include: Vaseline, Crisco, vegetable oil, hand lotion, baby oil, cold cream, massage oils, and whipped cream. Before you buy a lubricant, read the label and look for the words **"water-based."** A very **good option is a water-based lubricant containing a spermicide. Studies have shown that a spermicide called non-oxynol-9 kills HIV outside the body, and a condom lubricated with nonoxynol-9 may be your best bet.** (But don't use just the lubricant without a condom: Nonoxynol-9 alone can't keep you safe from HIV.)

You can also buy tubes of spermicidal foam, jelly, or cream, which a woman can put into her vagina with an applicator before vaginal intercourse, which is a lot like the way she would put in a tampon. The woman can also use a spermicide-filled contraceptive sponge or suppository. **Using this extra spermicide *in addition to* (never instead of) a condom is probably the best way to protect you and your partner from HIV and other STDs.** You'll find spermicides in most places where you find condoms on sale.

Some people are allergic to nonoxynol-9. If you get a rash or irritation from using this spermicide, check with your doctor to see if you're allergic. If you are, stick to plain latex condoms lubricated without nonoxynol-9.

how do I buy a condom?

You can find condoms in just about any drugstore, convenience store, or store with a pharmacy. Some places keep them behind the counter, where you'll have to ask for them. In other stores you'll find them displayed in a rack in front of the counter. It's best to stick with the major brands; they're the ones with the biggest displays and largest shelf space. Ask your friends about brand names that they have tried. If you're still not sure which condoms are major brands and you don't want to ask the store clerk, one teenager advised, "If you see a condom display and all but one condom of a particular brand are sold out—buy that last condom. If there's a whole stack of one brand and nobody's taken any off the rack, don't buy that brand."

You can usually buy condoms three to a packet

76 ———————————

for about $2, or in larger boxes of twelve for about $5 to $8. Some condoms cost a lot more than others. You simply pay for them at the checkout counter, no questions asked. Men and women of all ages buy condoms. You might feel embarrassed or a little nervous the first time you buy them, but there's no need to be. If you're a woman, remember the first time you bought tampons or sanitary napkins; you might have felt a little embarrassed the first time, but after a while buying them just became a part of your normal life. If it makes you feel more comfortable, try buying condoms in a different neighborhood from where you live.

"So You're Scared to Buy Rubbers? So Was I."

by Cassaundra Worrell

the big day came. I was going to buy some rubbers—and the only way I felt comfortable about it was to buy them in a different neighborhood.

I walked into Pathmark. I laughed to myself and figured no one had spotted me. Little did I know.

Beads of sweat formed across my brow. I waited as the area around the cash register slowly emptied before I approached. In a timid voice, I asked for the intimidating item.

A slow grin spread across the cashier's face. He then asked in a booming voice, "Lubricated or dry?"

When I said, "Yes," he realized he had yet another victim. He went for the kill.

By now I was ready to crack, because there was a line of people waiting behind me.

With that menacing grin, he screamed, "Ribbed or regular, colored or clear, flavored or without taste, lambskin or latex, edible or nonedible, and what size box?"

By this time I was ready to make in my pants.

"Regular, please, and the largest box you have." I added the last part so I would never have to come back.

I got the courage to look him in the face and saw his name tag: MIKE.

Mike's face got red from laughter as he told me the condoms were kept in the fourth aisle.

Am I the only one who has gone through the trauma of purchasing condoms?

My classmates who will read this may wonder how I managed. "Weren't you afraid that someone would laugh at you?" I certainly was, but I survived, and you can, too.

or makeup.

Don't you get tired of hearing your parents ask, "When are you going to grow up and accept your responsibilities?"

Having safer sex is one of the responsibilities that they're talking about. No matter what your friends may say, you're maturing. If you are thinking about having safer sex, you are a cut above the rest.

If you are having sex and you are thinking about buying condoms, you deserve a pat on the back—at least you're starting somewhere.

It was so degrading to have Mike laugh in my face and to have the people on line behind me look at me with "shame, shame, shame" written across their foreheads.

I know that buying a condom can be rough the first time, but at least you are taking responsibility for your actions, and it could just save your life.

Think about this as you ask for that box of condoms—**being embarrassed is much better than being dead.**

Food for thought: If you're afraid to buy any form of birth control, you shouldn't be having sex. ∎

You can also get condoms—sometimes free—from many STD clinics, health clinics, family-planning clinics, Planned Parenthood, AIDS information and support organizations, and drug treatment centers. Some men's and women's restrooms in bars, restaurants, hotels, and gas stations also sell them in vending machines. Some school districts give condoms to high school students who ask for them. If you do ask for a condom from your school clinic and they want to tell you how to use it, listen to them; you may learn something that could save your life.

how to use a condom

When you're using a condom, you've got to put it on once you get an erection (get hard) and **before** your penis touches your partner's vagina, anus, or mouth—and you must keep it on until after you come or decide to stop having sex. That's what I mean when I talk about using a condom "from start to finish." You can't wait until right before coming to put a condom on, because the pre-ejaculate, the clear fluid that oozes out of a man's penis soon after erection, may contain not only some sperm but also HIV and the germs that cause other STDs. The whole point of wearing a condom to prevent disease is to avoid contact of the penis with the vaginal area, anus, or mouth.

If you don't put the condom on properly, if you put it on too late, or if it comes off too soon, you and your partner will get much less protection from HIV or other STDs than you would otherwise have. Putting a condom on properly can be done quickly and easily, but it's not something anyone is born knowing how to do. So here's how to do it step by step:

80

eight simple steps to using a condom right

1) Keep a supply of latex condoms on hand. Store them in a cool, dry place out of direct sunlight. Light, heat, air, or any combination of them can ruin a latex condom. Don't keep condoms for too long in a wallet or pocket that can get too warm from the heat of your body, and don't let them sit in the glove compartment of a car or any other place where light or heat can ruin them.

2) Don't use condoms in damaged packages or condoms that show obvious signs of age (for example, those that seem brittle, sticky, or discolored). Many condom manufacturers put expiration dates on the packages. Throw a condom away once it has reached its expiration date. Stored properly, condoms can generally be used safely for at least three years from the time they are manufactured.

3) Open the package containing the condom only when you are ready to use it. If you open the package hours before you're ready to have sex, the condom can dry out and will be more likely to rip. If you have long or jagged fingernails, be especially careful not to puncture the condom when you open the package. Don't stretch or inflate the condom to test how strong it is, because this could actually weaken it.

4) Put the condom on when you get hard and before your penis touches your partner's body. When you open the package, the condom will be rolled up into a flat circle or oval. *Do not unroll it yet.* The center of that circle is the tip, the part that will cover the head of the penis. Condoms have either a bulblike tip at the end (called the "reservoir" or "receptacle") or a smooth tip. Either kind is fine. If the condom is dry, you may first want to put a drop of spermicidal lubricant into the tip, which will help the condom unroll more smoothly and increase the sensation for the wearer. (You can also add more lubricant even if the condom is already lubricated.)

Once you've taken the condom out of the package, gently pinch shut about a half-inch of the closed end between your thumb and index finger. You do this to squeeze out any air bubbles, which can cause condoms to break, and to make enough room for the semen to collect when you come.

Next, while still pinching shut the condom's closed end, place it against the tip of your penis. Then with your other hand unroll the condom down so that it covers the entire shaft of the penis all the way down to your testicles (or "balls"), down to the very base of the penis. (If you are uncircumcised, you should carefully pull back the foreskin of your penis before putting the condom on.) Add a few more drops of lubricant on the outside.

5) After you put the condom on, put some lubricant on the outside if necessary. Again, a lubricant containing spermicide is more effective than a condom alone for contracep-

HIV treatments work best when you start taking

tion, and protects you better against HIV and STDs. If you're having vaginal sex, using spermicidal foam, jelly, or cream in addition to the latex condom will give you the best protection of all. (If you're allergic, don't use nonoxynol-9.) Lubricants are also available in different flavors for oral sex. If you are having anal intercourse, you should definitely use more lubricant on the outside of the condom—and in and around the anus—because the anal opening is smaller, drier, and not as stretchy as the vaginal opening, and using more lubricant will make the condom less likely to rip when it enters the anus, and it will make the anus and rectum less likely to rip, too.

6) If you feel the condom slipping during sex, hold it at the base to keep it in place. If the condom comes off, put a new one on immediately before resuming sexual activity. To be safer, pull out before coming.

7) After you come or decide to stop having sex, hold the rim of the condom at the base of your penis while pulling out so the condom doesn't slip off. Pull out your penis while it's still hard so there's less chance that semen will leak or seep out of the condom. If you wait until your penis is soft, you might leave the condom behind, thereby exposing you and your partner to the other's blood, semen, or vaginal fluids.

8) Never, ever reuse a condom! After

you are done with the condom, wrap it in a paper towel, toilet paper, or napkin, and throw it away in the garbage. Don't flush it down the toilet; condoms float to the top of septic tanks. Never, ever use a condom more than once or share it with another person.

This may seem like a lot of steps, but in fact putting a condom on is pretty easy and takes only a few seconds. With very little practice, you can even put one on in the dark. You might want to practice when you are alone if you're afraid you might be embarrassed by not knowing how to do it in front of your sexual partner. Men can practice on themselves. Women can practice on any appropriately shaped fruit or vegetable.

What should I do if the condom breaks?

You should know that condom manufacturers inspect every lot of condoms they sell to be sure they meet safety standards. And a government agency called the Food and Drug Administration (FDA) checks constantly to make sure condom manufacturers are meeting those high standards of safety and effectiveness. So if you follow the above steps carefully, the condom is unlikely to break.

If the condom breaks while you're having sex, the man should pull out his penis immediately, remove the broken condom, wash his penis, genital area, and hands with soap and water, and put on another condom before starting to have sex again. If

Put a drop of lubricant inside the condom before you unroll it.

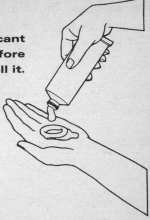

Pinch the top half-inch of the condom shut to squeeze out any air bubbles. Place it on your penis and start unrolling it.

Unroll the condom all the way down to the base of your penis.

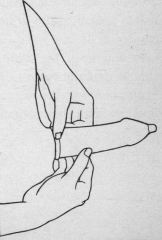

Always throw used condoms away. Never reuse a condom!

you've been having vaginal intercourse, the woman should put some spermicide into her vagina with an applicator. If the man has already come, you should probably not have any more vaginal sex because of the risk of spreading the semen around. If the man hasn't come yet, he can put on a new condom with spermicide and keep on having vaginal sex. The woman should **not** douche, as douching can cause small rips in the lining of the vagina, and HIV could enter her body through these openings.

86

fifteen lousy excuses for not using a condom

▶ **1) "If I carry a condom, people will think I'm easy or looking for sex."**
Carrying a condom doesn't mean you're looking to sleep around. Many women worry that if they carry a condom, it means they're not "good girls." Carrying a condom means you care enough about yourself and your partner to protect both of you. Most people don't plan in advance the first time they have sex—so always be prepared with a condom.

▶ **2) "I'm embarrassed to buy them."**
Everybody buys condoms—men and women. Manufacturers even make condoms meant to appeal especially to women. No one will ask you any questions, and no one cares how old you are. If you find it truly embarrassing, you can go to a different part of town, where no one knows you, to buy them or you can ask a friend to buy them for you or you can get them out of restroom vending machines or from health clinics, where you can just take them free from a bowl without having to ask anybody. Don't let embarrassment stop you from doing what you need to do to protect your health.

▶ **3) "I'm afraid I'll insult my partner."**
Being prepared with a condom doesn't mean you think your partner is someone who sleeps around

it's also okay to choose not to act on them.

87

a lot or uses drugs—or even that you think he or she has HIV or another STD. If you think your partner will be offended if you bring the subject up, just explain that you care enough about him or her to want to protect you both.

▶ **4) "I know my partner isn't infected. We love each other, so we don't need to use a condom."** You may **never** know whether your partner is infected. Don't put your head in the sand and say, "My boyfriend would never do anything to hurt me." What if he doesn't know he has it? **You** are the one who's responsible for your own health—no one else. Even people who are in love can get HIV from each other. When your emotions are making the decisions for you instead of your head, that's when you're putting yourself at risk. Don't use your genitals for a brain. If you trust each other enough to have sex, you should care enough to protect each other's health.

▶ **5) "I forgot to bring one. I'll take a chance just this once."** That's one chance you may live to regret. Remember: You can get HIV from having unprotected sex with an infected person just once. Why take a chance? If you don't want to stop and get a condom, do sexy things that don't involve genital contact with blood, semen, or vaginal fluids. (See the list on page 72.)

6) "Sex doesn't feel as good with condoms." You lose very little sensation when you wear a condom. Putting some water-based lubricant in the tip before putting them on makes condoms feel even more natural to some men. Many men find that they take longer to come when they wear a condom, so they and their partner can enjoy sex longer. So condoms are especially good for men who have trouble with premature ejaculation (coming too soon).

7) "I want my sex to be spontaneous." Some people think that planning for sex by carrying a condom makes the sex less fun or less romantic. Others say it "takes away their freedom." This simply isn't true. Spontaneous sex isn't necessarily better sex. In fact, you might enjoy sex more if you don't have to worry about whether you'll get HIV. You and your partner can even make putting a condom on part of the fun of having sex.

8) "I'm too drunk (or high) to deal with a condom." It's your responsibility to take charge of protecting yourself against HIV. You're the one who has to stay in control. Alcohol and drugs can affect your judgment, so you're less able or willing to protect yourself during sex. You can get HIV from having unprotected sex just one time with an infected partner. Is it worth the risk? You can have great safer sex without being drunk or high. Stay in control.

▶ **9) "My church says it's a sin to use a condom."** Thinking about your religious values and what your conscience says is an important part of making a decision about having sex. Some people think that the values they learn from their religion don't help very much when it comes to thinking about sex and condoms. Talking with your parents, priest, minister, or rabbi can sometimes help you sort through the confusion. But if you then decide not to follow your religious community's advice about sex, follow its teaching about taking care of yourself and others. Most religions teach that we need to care for others the way we want to be cared for. You would want your partner to protect you from HIV, so you need to make the moral commitment to protect your partner. And that means using condoms every time you have sex.

▶ **10) "It's not macho to use a condom."** Some men think it's not macho to use a condom, or they feel that if a partner asks them to use one, that's an insult to their machismo. Being prepared for sex has nothing to do with your masculinity. It just shows that you're smart and that you care. What's so macho about getting HIV?

90

11) "Condoms are expensive." A condom costs less than a fast-food burger, and you can even get condoms free in a lot of places. Isn't your health—or your life—worth the price of a burger? A condom is certainly cheaper than the cost of any illness you might get if you don't use one.

12) "We always use condoms. Can't we forget them just this once?" This is the "time off for good behavior" argument. You're not protected against HIV or other STDs unless you use a condom each and every time you have sex.

13) "If you think you're going to get some sex, you won't. So I don't carry a condom." People who think this way think that carrying a condom will somehow "jinx" their chances to have sex. If that's your attitude, it says you're willing to put yourself and your partner at risk. What's more, the notion itself is a myth. It's just not true.

14) "We got so carried away, by the time we thought about condoms, it was too late to bother." Condoms don't have to stop the flow of your lovemaking, and with a little creativity you can make putting one on part of the pleasure. If you don't think you've got the strength to stop things and walk over to the bathroom, where you keep the condoms, then don't keep them in the bathroom! Keep them near the bed or in your purse or jacket. Just keep them handy—and use them.

▶ **15) "My partner will think I don't trust him or her."** You've got to separate the issues of trust and protection; they don't have anything to do with each other. Safer sex isn't a barricade to trust. You're both in this thing together, but each of you has responsibility for his or her own body.

I know what it's like; I've used some of these excuses myself. No excuse is worth risking your health.

safer sex for mouth-to-vagina and mouth-to-anus sex

You can get syphilis and herpes from mouth-to-vagina sex. You can get herpes, syphilis, hepatitis, and intestinal infections from mouth-to-anus sex. A few people have gotten HIV from either kind of sex. That means you should practice safer sex if you want to have mouth-to-vagina sex (cunnilingus) or mouth-to-anus sex (anilingus).

The problem is, although latex condoms have been tested and proven effective for preventing HIV and other STDs from getting passed during mouth-to-penis sex, *no* materials or devices have been specifically manufactured, tested, and approved for other types of oral sex. That means that scientists *can't recommend or endorse anything* for these kinds of oral sex because nothing has been scientifically proven to be effective. The best they can do is suggest some items that are known to be barriers to moisture and remind people that we don't yet know whether they're effective in preventing STDs, including HIV.

However, some people have used three different types of items for anilingus and cunnilingus: household plastic wrap (the kind you use to wrap food in); dental dams (square pieces of latex, four or six inches long, used by dentists during oral surgery); and cut-open and flattened condoms. The effectiveness of these items in blocking body fluids that contain HIV or other STDs would depend on their adequately covering the area of contact and not being punctured. Since none of these items can be sterilized, they should never be used more than once.

Of these three items, household plastic wrap has the advantage of being larger, cheaper, more readily available, and somewhat resistant to puncture. The plastic film used for trash, sandwich, grocery, and dry cleaning bags *is not the same as* household plastic wraps. These items are weaker, more porous (full of holes that can let bacteria and viruses through), and easier to rip and puncture, and should **not** be used in oral sex.

The latex in dental dams is not the same kind of

latex as in latex condoms; it can have thin spots and pinholes. Some people snip the tops off condoms and cut them lengthwise and lay them flat for oral sex. The latex from condoms or latex surgical gloves conceivably could be somewhat effective in preventing infected blood, semen, or vaginal fluids from getting into an uninfected partner's mucous membranes during anilingus or cunnilingus, provided the latex wasn't punctured and that it completely covered the area of contact.

People who use dentals dams, cut-up condoms, or plastic wrap sometimes spread a water-based lubricant on the side that will go against the vagina or anus, then hold it in place over the area so that one partner's mouth, lips, or tongue doesn't touch the other partner's vaginal or anal area.

Again, since no studies have proven the effectiveness of any of these materials and methods, scientists can't endorse them or recommend them. Using some kind of barrier during anilingus or cunnilingus is probably safer than using no barrier at all. What's important is that you know the risks and make your own decision.

Is household plastic wrap a safe substitute for a condom?

I've heard that some people use household plastic wrap instead of latex condoms. Again, there is no research that shows plastic wrap can stop HIV. So don't use it; latex condoms are cheap (or free) and available.

If you don't have a condom, you and your partner can give each other massages or engage in another safe activity rather than have sex.

if I have HIV, can I have sex?
Yes, but I have to remind you again, there are few absolute guarantees in life. I think you should tell your partner you have HIV before you have sex so you can make choices together. If you practice safer sex every time by using a latex condom from start to finish, you can greatly reduce your chance of giving HIV to someone else. You can also greatly reduce your chances of being reinfected by someone with the virus or of getting another STD. The guidelines should be the same whether you have HIV or not: **safer sex every time.** You should also remember that there's no research on how effective barriers are for anilingus and cunnilingus.

can I have safer sex with a partner who's infected with HIV?
Again, there are few absolute guarantees in life, but using a latex condom every time you have sex can greatly reduce your chance of getting HIV or another STD from your partner or giving your partner another STD if you're infected. There's no research on how effective barriers are for anilingus and cunnilingus.

how do I know whether what I'm doing is risky behavior?

I've tried to give you some clear guidelines in this book, but if ever you're in doubt, here's how to figure it out yourself.

Remember: HIV is spread through blood, semen, vaginal fluids (including menstrual blood), and breast milk. Risky sexual behavior is behavior that could allow any of those fluids to enter the mucous membranes that line the vagina, rectum, mouth, or tip of the penis. The riskiest sexual activity is probably unprotected anal sex, because the blood vessels are closest to the surface there. Other risky behavior includes sharing needles (or other sharp objects that can pierce the skin) that have been contaminated with the virus.

In some sex play, one person puts a finger or fist into another person's anus or puts a dildo (penis-shaped sex toy) or vibrator into another person's vagina or anus. These activities can spread HIV if the virus goes from the blood, sperm, or vaginal secretions of one person onto the finger, fist, dildo, or other sex toy and from there to the uninfected person's mucous membranes in the vagina, tip of the penis, rectum, or mouth. Putting a fist into someone else's rectum is very likely to cause small rips in the lining of the rectum. For this reason, some people wear latex

risky sex is any sexual behavior that could get

gloves or "finger cots" (which cover just the fingers) that they've lubricated with a spermicidal jelly or foam if they're going to engage in such activities. There is no research to prove whether this provides effective protection. You have to make your own decision here. If you use a dildo, put a latex condom and spermicidal lubricant on it, and throw the condom away after you've used it once. Some people who use other sex toys wash them thoroughly with a bleach solution after using them on just one person; unfortunately, there's no research to prove this is effective protection. Again, make your own decision.

If you're still not sure whether something you want to do is risky, **stop. Then call** your local source for AIDS information (see the State-by-State Directory of Resources at the back of this book) or the toll-free CDC National HIV and AIDS Hotline at 1 (800) 342-AIDS. For Spanish-speaking persons, call La Linea Nacional de SIDA: 1 (800) 344-SIDA. For hearing-impaired persons, call TDD 1 (800) 243-7889.

Safer sex and birth control

because latex condoms, when used properly, are effective at preventing both pregnancy and HIV and other STDs, you may think that other methods of birth control

blood, vaginal fluids, or semen inside your or

might also protect against HIV. *This is not true.* No other form of birth control helps prevent HIV infection, because the condom is the only method that protects the lining of the vagina from coming into contact with the penis or secretions from the penis.

▶ The birth control pill, IUD, diaphragm, cervical cap, and fertility-awareness methods (such as the basal body temperature method or vaginal mucus system) don't protect at all against HIV or other STDs. If you use any of these methods of birth control, you should also use a latex condom with spermicide to give yourself the best protection against HIV and other STDs.

▶ Contraceptive foams, creams, jellies, suppository capsules, and films; contraceptive sponges; and the spermicides used with the diaphragm and cervical cap don't give you enough protection from HIV and other STDs, so *never* rely on them alone. Always use a latex

someone else's body.

condom with spermicide along with any of these methods.

▶ Vaginal douching is not only a poor method of contraception, but it may actually make it easier for you to get HIV or another STD. *Don't douche.*

▶ Withdrawal (pulling the penis out before you come) doesn't offer any protection against HIV and other STDs. You should use a latex condom with spermicide from start to finish.

▶ Voluntary sterilization is the most effective birth control of all, but it doesn't offer you any protection against HIV and other STDs. If you're going to have sex, you will still need to use a condom with spermicide to help protect yourself against HIV and other STDs.

what do I tell a partner who's not into safer sex?

Look, you've got to be strong. This is your life. Make up your mind that it's not a question of whether anyone is "into" safer sex or not. Your basic message to your partner has to be: **"It's safer sex or no**

sex." It's okay to say, "I'm really embarrassed to be talking to you about this right now, but this is just something we've got to do." If your partner tells you he or she is a virgin who doesn't do drugs so you both don't need to use protection, you've just got to be strong and say, "This condom is for your protection and mine."

A lot of women have a hard time telling a man that he's got to wear a condom, but you've got to do it in order to take care of yourself. If you choose to be sexually active, always carry a latex condom for your own protection. Be sure that the man puts the condom on as soon as he gets hard and before his penis touches your body. It might be easier for you and more enjoyable for your partner if you can find some sexy way to help him with the condom—you might want to put it on for him. Maybe your friends have some good ideas about how to make using a condom more exciting.

Some people like to show off the fact that they carry a condom around, because they think it makes them look cool. But it's definitely *not* cool if you don't use it. Or, as one teenager put it, "I don't care if it's cool. I'm using a condom to protect my own butt."

If someone won't have sex with you with a condom, you're better off letting that person go. This can be really hard to do. But face it. If this person really cared about you, he or she would want to protect your health by practicing safer sex. If you decide you want

being in a monogamous relationship doesn't

to spend the rest of your life with this partner, you may eventually prove to each other, with the help of your doctor, that it's safe to have sex without a condom. Or if one of you is infected, you will be glad you protected the other and can keep protecting him or her.

Remember: Practice safer sex each and every time you have sex.

"I have HIV."

dawn Marcal was 25 when she was interviewed. This is her story.

When I was a teenager, what I really wanted was to find a great guy and fall in love. The big mistake I made was in thinking that if I had sex with someone, he would love me. I believed it when someone said that by having sex we'd become closer, that the relationship would become stronger. I can tell you, 99 percent of the time that doesn't happen.

I got hurt. I tried to pretend that I didn't care, that it didn't hurt. But I couldn't. I tried all kinds of crazy things. I tried all kinds of drugs. When I was seventeen, I tried IV drugs.

Then something funny happened. I grew up. I stopped trying drugs. I finished high school. I went to college for a little while and ended up with a good job in an office.

I met this really wonderful guy and we fell in love. I told him all about my experiences when I was a teenager, and he didn't mind. He said to me, "Dawn, you were just a teenager. Everyone does crazy things when they're young. That's all in the past." I was relieved.

We got married and started trying to get pregnant. After six months it happened. Oh! To feel that baby move inside was like heaven! I loved to feel that baby move around and watch my tummy change shapes.

There were some complications with my labor, and my daughter swallowed some fluid while she was being born. She developed pneumonia and was in the hospital a week. We named her Lindsey.

Lindsey got better and came home. We then had about three months of "normal babyhood," which means sleepless nights and breast-feeding and changing icky diapers, learning how to be a good mommy, and falling so in love with my beautiful baby.

Everything seemed okay those first three months. The only thing I noticed was that whenever Lindsey cried real hard, she'd turn kind of blue around her mouth. I took her to the doctor a couple of times, but they always said she was fine. They said I was just a new mom and that I worried too much. I was relieved.

When Lindsey was three months old, I took her for her first vaccination. We saw a different doctor this time, and he saw her turn blue. "Oh, something's wrong," he said. "We'll have to hospitalize her and find out what's going on." So she went into the hospital for three weeks.

She had viral pneumonia. At first, the doctors couldn't figure out what kind of virus she had and one of the doctors asked me if I or my husband did drugs. I automatically said no, because we didn't. Then I realized why she was asking me that. So I said to her, "Why? You don't think it's that virus, do you?" I wouldn't say the word "AIDS."

"Oh no," she said. "We ask everyone that nowadays." I was relieved, and my baby got better and we came home. About a month later, they wanted to put her back in the hospital for some more tests because she wasn't getting completely well. She wasn't gaining weight.

I had really been thinking about what that doctor had asked me. When I was a teenager you hadn't heard about AIDS. Everyone thought it was just a gay men's disease. But in the last few years, we'd heard more and more about it. I knew that I had done things when I was a teenager that would put me at risk for being exposed to the virus. I had had unsafe sex and I had tried IV drugs. I felt I had to go for the AIDS test for my baby's sake.

I went for the test and spent two really horrible weeks waiting for the test results. Every night I would pray, "Please, God, if I have to have this thing, fine. If I have to die, fine. I can accept that. I made the mistakes. Don't make her have to pay for my mistakes!"

Well, obviously, my test came back positive. My husband went to be tested and we were really lucky, because he tested negative. He hadn't caught the virus from me.

My daughter tested positive. When Lindsey was a year old, we realized she had AIDS.

We did everything we knew how to save her life and make her as happy and as comfortable as possible. She was on AZT. We took her to a homeopathic doctor—a doctor who works with nature and herbs. We took her to a nutritionist, who put her on vitamin therapy. We even took her to see a Catholic priest who was supposed to be a faith healer. We did everything we knew how. It just wasn't meant to be. When she was eighteen months old, she died.

Lindsey was the most amazing person I have ever met. She taught me so much. Lindsey taught me how to be strong. How to fight. How to laugh and smile even when it's hard. She taught me how to enjoy every moment that I have and to never give up. My baby was the first thing I ever did that I really felt proud of myself for. I was a damn good mommy! And by being Lindsey's mommy, I learned how to live. She gave and gives me the strength to go on. ∎

CHAPTER 4

how to **protect yourself** from other Sexually Transmitted Diseases

everyone talks so much about HIV and AIDS these days that you may not think you need to worry about anything else when you have sex. In fact, HIV is one of more than 20 sexually transmitted diseases (STDs). Each year about 12 million people get STDs, including 3 million teenagers. HIV is actually pretty hard to get compared with most of these other STDs.

These STDs range from annoying to life-threatening if left untreated. But all of them are bad for you. Some STDs can make you sterile, so you can't have children. Others can destroy your heart or liver or brain. Some can make it more likely that you'll get certain kinds of cancer later in life. *Not all of them can be cured, but they can all be prevented.*

Let's talk about the seven most common STDs, how to recognize the symptoms, and how they're treated.

1) chlamydia ("cla-MID-ee-ah")
what are the symptoms?
Each year about 4 million men and women get chlamydia, the most common STD in the United States. Chlamydia is caused by germs that can get spread during vaginal, anal, and oral sex or from the vagina to a newborn baby during childbirth and, rarely, from genitals to the hand to the eye.

Most people who get chlamydia don't know it. Sometimes it can cause an unusual discharge from the penis or vagina or cause pain during sex or burning during urination, but three out of four people don't have **any** symptoms until the infection is fairly serious. Symptoms of serious infection are fever, abdominal pain, nausea, bleeding from the vagina, and arthritis.

how is it diagnosed?
Doctors can test secretions from the penis or vagina during an office visit. If you are sexually active, you

should be tested for chlamydia every year. If you have chlamydia, you should tell anyone you've had sex with so he or she can get tested and treated. Otherwise, you may be infected again. A lot of people learn they've got chlamydia only after their partners test positive.

how is it treated?

An antibiotic, usually tetracycline, will cure the infection in a week or two. If you're pregnant or think you could be, tell your doctor. Tetracycline can harm your fetus, so you'll have to be treated with a different antibiotic, called erythromycin. In women, chlamydia can cause bladder infections and serious pelvic inflammatory disease (PID), which can lead to ectopic pregnancy (see page 110) and sterility. If you have chlamydia, don't douche, because that could make it easier for you to get PID. Men can get chlamydia, too. It can lead to arthritis in both men and women. In infants, chlamydia can cause eye infections and pneumonia.

Women who get chlamydia while using the IUD (a contraceptive device that is inserted into the uterus) are more likely to develop PID, so talk to your doctor and ask whether the IUD is the best method of birth control for you. Some studies show that women who take birth control pills are more likely to get chlamydia, but they are not more likely to get PID because of chlamydia.

you can't tell if someone has HIV

2) genital warts
what are the symptoms?

Every year about 500,000 to 1 million people get genital warts, also known as condyloma. Twenty to 30 percent of sexually active Americans are infected with the virus that causes genital warts. In some cities, half of all sexually active teenagers have this STD. Teenage girls under age eighteen are at the greatest risk. Genital warts can be spread through vaginal, anal, and oral sex, and women can pass the virus to newborns during childbirth. If you've been infected, small bumps may start to grow in or near your vagina, penis, or rectum, although they may not appear until one to three months after you've been infected. Because they can grow inside your vagina, penis, or rectum, you may not be aware of the warts until they cause itching or pain during sex. Some people can have genital warts and never know it. If you're a woman, the warts will grow more quickly if you're pregnant or have another STD. Genital warts can block the openings of the vagina, anus, or penis and become quite uncomfortable.

how are they diagnosed?

Doctors can diagnose genital warts during a standard medical examination. However, you can have the virus without any visible sign.

how are they treated?

Doctors usually remove them by freezing or burning them off, applying chemical solutions, or, more rarely,

just by looking at him or her.

surgery. However, treatment does not eliminate the virus. Genital warts can recur (come back), so you may have to be treated more than once. If you have genital warts, make sure you inform your partner. Genital warts can also have other very serious consequences. Many people who have the virus that causes genital warts also have related viruses that can lead to cancer of the cervix, vulva, or penis. Doctors say that women who have unprotected sex before the age of twenty increase their risk of cervical cancer. Any woman who has ever had genital warts should have a Pap smear every year to check for signs of cancer.

3) pelvic inflammatory disease (PID)
what are the symptoms?
Every year about 1 million women contract PID. Both gonorrhea and chlamydia can cause PID. Many women who get PID never know it, because they have no symptoms. Others may have fever, nausea, vomiting, chills, pain in the lower abdomen, pain during sex, spotting and pain between menstrual periods or during urination, and heavy bleeding during menstrual periods. You can get PID when STD infection spreads from your vagina to your fallopian tubes, uterus, and ovaries. The tubes become scarred, so when you are ready to become pregnant, a fertilized egg could start to develop there instead of in the uterus (this is called an ectopic or tubal pregnancy). This destroys the developing embryo, puts your life in danger, and requires an operation.

110

how is it diagnosed?

PID is diagnosed by a doctor during a routine pelvic exam. Unfortunately, many women don't realize they've been infected and don't seek treatment early enough to avoid the complications of PID. If you're diagnosed with PID, you should have your sexual partner tested and treated for STDs so you won't be reinfected.

how is it treated?

PID is treated with antibiotics, bed rest, and sexual abstinence. You may need to be hospitalized. You may need surgery to remove infected, scarred tissue or to repair or remove your fallopian tubes or uterus. Treated or untreated, PID can lead to sterility, ectopic pregnancy, and chronic pain. The more times you've had PID, the more likely it is that you'll have these problems. Even if your PID was treated successfully and you don't have any more symptoms, your fallopian tubes may be so scarred that you will still be sterile.

4) gonorrhea ("gon-uh-REE-uh")
what are the symptoms?

In 1990, almost 700,000 people were treated for gonorrhea, which you can get from vaginal, anal, or oral sex. Men usually—but not always—notice symptoms about a week after having sex with someone who's infected; you'll probably notice a puslike secretion coming from your penis and a burning sensation when you urinate. But women who get infected with gonorrhea usually don't have **any** symptoms. Some may have a green or yellowish-green discharge from the vagina, swelling or tenderness around the vagina, and painful urination, and they might feel sharp pain—not menstrual cramps—during the first menstrual period after they've been infected. Most women, however, won't have any idea that they're infected until the infection is serious enough to cause high fever, severe abdominal pain, and other complications, including PID.

how is it diagnosed?
Doctors diagnose gonorrhea by examining discharges from the penis or vagina and by taking cultures from the cervix, throat, urethra, or rectum. Since most women and some men never show any symptoms of gonorrhea, you should get tested for gonorrhea if you have any of the above symptoms or if you've had unprotected sex.

how is it treated?
Gonorrhea is treated with penicillin or other antibiotics. Many people with gonorrhea also have chlamydia and need to be treated for both infections. If left untreated, gonorrhea can cause sterility, arthritis, and heart problems. In women it can also cause pelvic inflammatory disease (PID) (see above). If you're pregnant and have gonorrhea, your infection can cause you to deliver your baby prematurely or can

know whether someone is infected unless

even kill the fetus, so it's important to get tested and treated early.

5) genital herpes ("HER-peas")
what are the symptoms?

Every year anywhere from 200,000 to 500,000 people get herpes, which can be spread by vaginal, anal, and oral sex—and even by kissing and touching each other's genitals. The virus causes painful, burning, blistery sores on the vagina, cervix, penis, mouth, anus, or anywhere else the herpes virus may have entered the body. The sores usually appear within ten days after infection. Scabs gradually form over them and the sores clear up on their own after about three weeks. During that time you can also have flulike symptoms—headache, fever, muscle aches, and swollen glands. Herpes can be spread from one partner to another, or from one part of the body to another, whenever contact is made with an active herpes virus sore. Herpes is most contagious (meaning you can catch it most easily) from the time the sores appear until they are completely healed and the scabs have fallen off. Unfortunately, some people may be contagious even when they have **no** symptoms.

how is it diagnosed?

Herpes can be diagnosed by a doctor during a medical examination, or a laboratory can analyze the fluid from the sores.

how is it treated?

There is no cure for herpes. Between 10 and 20 million Americans have genital herpes. The virus will live in your body for the rest of your life, and you may have recurrences, or "flare-ups," where you'll break out in more sores, though these recurrences are usually less severe. Some people have many recurrences; others have none. Some people are more likely to have recurrences when they're stressed out or feeling run-down. If you have herpes sores, wash your hands frequently and don't touch the sores. If you do touch them by accident, wash your hands immediately. Be particularly careful when handling contact lenses, since your eyes can get infected easily. Some people take a drug called acyclovir to prevent recurrences. Talk to your doctor to see if you should take acyclovir. He or she may prescribe medication to ease your symptoms.

If you have active herpes during childbirth the infection can seriously harm your newborn baby. Your doctor may therefore perform a cesarean section to avoid infecting the newborn baby.

6) hepatitis b

what are the symptoms?

Every year about 300,000 people get hepatitis B, a contagious illness that you can get from vaginal, anal, and oral sex, and from sharing contaminated needles with someone who is infected. Many people who get hepatitis B have no symptoms; others may feel ex-

114 —

tremely tired all the time, and they can have headaches, fever, nausea, loss of appetite, dark frothy urine, light-colored stools, and tenderness in the upper abdomen, and their skin and the whites of their eyes will turn yellowish (this is called jaundice).

how is it diagnosed?
Hepatitis B is diagnosed by a physical examination and a blood test.

how is it treated?
There is no cure for hepatitis B; 90 to 95 percent of people who have been infected recover completely, but the rest can get severe liver disease and even die from the infection. People with hepatitis should not donate blood. The blood banks test all blood and throw away any donations contaminated with hepatitis. A vaccine can protect you against hepatitis B. If you have HIV, you should talk to your doctor about getting the vaccine, because hepatitis B can be much more serious for people with HIV. The vaccine is also recommended for health-care workers (doctors, nurses, dentists, etc.).

7) syphilis ("SIF-uh-lis")
what are the symptoms?
Maybe you thought that no one got syphilis anymore. In fact, every year in the United States there are up to 100,000 cases of syphilis, which can be spread by vaginal, anal, or oral sex. Syphilis has three stages of

symptoms. In the first stage, which many people don't notice, it causes a painless sore, known as a chancre, to appear within two to twelve weeks of infection. This sore can appear on the penis, or inside or just outside the vagina, or in or around the mouth or anus. The clear liquid that oozes from the sore is very infectious, which means that if you come into contact with it, you can get syphilis very easily. The sore usually goes away after a few weeks, even without treatment. But that doesn't mean the infection goes away. If not treated, the disease goes into a second stage several weeks or months later. The symptoms usually include a rash but also fever, aches, and hair loss. If not treated, the disease goes into a third and final stage of symptoms, the most serious of all. The final stage of syphilis can cause severe mental illness, heart disease, damage to the nervous system (making it difficult to walk), and blindness.

how is it diagnosed?

If sores are present, a doctor can examine the liquid from them under a microscope. Otherwise, a blood test is needed to tell whether you have syphilis. Anybody who is sexually active and who develops genital sores or whose partner is infected should get tested for syphilis.

oil-based lubricants can make a condom break.

how is it treated?

Syphilis can be treated and stopped at any stage with antibiotics, but treatment cannot undo any damage that might already have occurred.

One of the greatest risks of syphilis is that a pregnant woman who is infected will pass the disease to her unborn baby. If untreated, syphilis can cause stillbirth or birth defects, but pregnant women with syphilis can be given medication to prevent damage to the fetus.

if you're sexually active, you're at risk for an STD

▶ **Remember:** Many people, especially women, who get STDs **never** have any symptoms, so they don't know they're infected. So if you're sexually active, **practice safer sex** and **get regular medical checkups.**

▶ If you have an STD that causes open sores on your genitals, such as herpes, you're more likely to get HIV from having sex with someone who's infected. If your partner has HIV (and you probably won't know that) and has herpes or any other STD, your chances of getting HIV go up considerably.

▶ If you think you have an STD, don't think the problem's gone if the symptoms go away. You could still be infected. If you've got syphilis, you'll never be able to undo the damage that happened before you got treatment, so don't delay.

▶ You can't ever become immune to an STD, meaning that you can get it again and again. If you get an STD, you should tell anybody you've been having sex with and be sure he or she gets tested. You both need treatment or you could keep reinfecting each other and/or others.

▶ Getting an STD now could mean health problems for you later in life, especially if you put off getting treatment.

how to protect yourself against STDs

1) If you can wait for sex—wait.

2) Be aware that the more people you have unprotected sex with, the more likely it is that you'll be exposed to an STD. As with HIV, you can never be completely sure whether someone has an STD just by asking him or her.

3) Always use a latex condom and spermicide from start to finish when you have vaginal, anal, or oral sex. Remember the rule: Safer sex each and every time you have sex.

4) Be alert for symptoms. If you have any unusual discharges, sores, blisters, lumps, bumps, itching, or pain in, on, or around your penis, vagina, or anus—or if you've had sex with someone you even think might have an STD—go to your doctor or clinic for a checkup. If you're in any doubt, it's always wiser to get it checked out. In the meantime, don't have sex.

5) Never try to diagnose or treat

118

safer sex or no sex, every time.

yourself. People who do so generally end up in a doctor's office or clinic anyway, but in the meantime, the infection's gotten worse and you may have spread it to someone else. You have no way of knowing how serious your infection is—life-threatening infections can have the same symptoms as mild ones. Only a doctor or health clinic can tell for sure what the problem is. Plenty of clinics and organizations can examine and test you in complete confidence, so nobody will ever know you have an STD—except the people you've had sex with, whom you should tell. Check your Yellow Pages under "birth control clinics" or "clinics" or check your city or state health department to find out where you can go for confidential testing and treatment.

6) If you're sexually active, get a regular medical checkup. Since you can have an STD and **never** have any symptoms, don't wait until you suspect you have a problem to get a checkup. Plan to go at least once or twice a year to make sure you're not infected. Women should have an annual breast and pelvic exam, including a Pap test, and should not douche, have sex, or use any vaginal medications before the pelvic exam, since this could make it harder for the doctor to examine vaginal secretions that may indicate you have an infection. If tests show you have an STD, tell your partner so he or she can be treated and you don't keep reinfecting each other.

7) Be straight with the doctor or

clinic. Find a doctor or some other health-care worker you feel comfortable with, and be completely honest with the person giving you the checkup. Tell him or her if you're having any kind of symptoms; if you're having sex with more than one person; if you're having vaginal, anal, or oral sex; if you're shooting drugs; if you think you could be pregnant. Many symptoms of STDs can be mistaken for other ailments. If you don't give the doctor all the information, you might not get the right treatment. Remember: The medical person isn't there to judge you; he or she is there to treat you, so don't be embarrassed to tell the truth. If someone does embarrass you, find a new doctor.

if you're being treated for an STD

▶ Make the connection: You got the STD through risky behavior—you could get HIV the same way.

▶ Tell the doctor who examines you if you're taking any other drugs, medications, herbal teas, or other home remedies. Such remedies might interact in ways that could cause problems your doctor needs to know about.

▶ If you're pregnant or think you might be, tell your doctor. Some medications can harm the fetus. Your doctor will prescribe a safe medication for you and your baby.

▶ If the doctor prescribes vaginal suppositories and some of the medication drips out, don't use tampons to absorb it. Don't even use tampons

120

for your period while you're being treated. They can soak up the medication before it has a chance to work. Use panty liners or sanitary napkins instead.

▶ Take all the medication prescribed, even after the symptoms disappear. Remember: You can have no symptoms and still be infected. If you don't finish the medication, the infection will probably come right back.

▶ Don't share your medications with anyone else. If you share your prescription with somebody else, each of you will get only half of what you need to knock out the infection, and neither of you will be cured.

▶ It may not be safe to have sex—even with a latex condom and spermicide—while you're being treated. Ask the doctor who's treating you if it's okay. You don't want to give your infection to anyone else or get another STD—and it's easier to get another STD if you already have one.

▶ Make sure that your partner gets treated, too, so you don't keep reinfecting each other.

▶ If the doctor or clinic tells you to come back for a follow-up exam, keep the appointment. Only the doctor or clinic can tell for sure if the infection's completely gone.

Remember: All STDs are trouble. Just because most of them can be cured easily and they aren't as threatening as HIV doesn't mean you shouldn't take them seriously. For your health right now, for your health later in life, and for the health of the people you have sex with, always practice safer sex and get regular checkups.

"I have HIV."

Joe B. Franco was 29 years old at the time of this interview.

A Mexican-American, Joe was raised in Denver, Colorado, and then did undergraduate work at Ohio State in Columbus, Ohio. From age 17 until 21, he went to school, worked at four part-time jobs, played serious volleyball, and studied. Joe, who is gay, believes he got HIV during that time, even though he was too wrapped up in school and work to be very sexually active, "because no one had ever educated me about safer sex in Denver or Columbus. No one even talked about it. If you stop and think about it, if you don't know what high-risk behavior is and you do risky things for a long time, you're probably getting infected with HIV more than once."

In 1985 Joe moved to New York City, and his awareness of AIDS went up considerably. He started doing volunteer work in 1987, counseling

about 4 million people get chlamydia every year.

women, people of color, people with chemical dependencies, and adolescents on AIDS prevention. Then, in December 1987, he starting coming down with respiratory infections. He took an anonymous HIV antibody test in the spring of 1988 and learned he had the virus. In 1989 he was diagnosed as having AIDS.

Today Joe continues his work as an AIDS educator. He organizes communities for AIDS prevention through VOCAL, Voices of Color Against AIDS. His main message? "Practice safer sex. Use latex condoms every time." Many men, he points out, have "this big rap against using condoms. They complain that having sex with a rubber is like taking a shower in a raincoat. But excuses won't protect you or your partner."

Joe also tells people "not to point the finger at kids and tell them that they have to grow up and act like adults. A lot of adults aren't practicing safer sex either. We *all* have to practice safer sex; adults have to teach kids by the power of example. It's what you do, not how old you are when you do it." ∎

CHAPTER 5
if you do
drugs or
drink

When it comes to drugs and HIV, you have the power to choose.

I've always been against drugs. You've heard the lectures. In the end it's your choice. But I think doing drugs is a great way to waste your time and eat up your money. It can make you an addict and land you in jail and keep you from your dreams. You can get HIV from sharing needles with someone who's infected. Also, when you do drugs—or drink alcohol—you don't think straight. And when you don't think straight, you are tempted to take stupid chances—like having unsafe sex.

You're going to go to parties where temptations of all kinds will be around. Don't get into a situation in which you get high or drunk and lose your self-control. The first time somebody offers you a drug, remember that he or she doesn't have the right to push you into taking it. Don't fall for one of those lame lines that drugs will solve all your problems or make you better at sex or give you a new reason for living. Drugs don't do you any good under any circumstances. It's your choice to say, "No, thanks."

If you're already doing drugs or drinking, get some help and stop. You don't have to go through it alone, and if you're taking serious drugs, you're definitely going to need some help. You are not alone; thousands of others just like you are also trying to get help, and help is out there. Call the number at the end of this chapter.

if you shoot drugs

If you're mainlining or skin-popping drugs, you're at risk for more than HIV. You're at risk for overdosing and hepatitis, too. You're also more at risk for dying from drug overdoses or drug-induced violence. If you've started exchanging sex for drugs or money to support your habit, you're exposing yourself to the risk of HIV and other STDs from your customers ("johns") as well as the threat of violence. And if you're a woman who shoots drugs and you get pregnant, you're risking your unborn child's life as well as your own.

Shooting drugs is one of the most dangerous things you can do to yourself. Please get help. Get into a drug treatment or a detox program. Call the number at the end of this chapter for help.

If you shoot drugs, there are some things you can do to reduce your risk of HIV. **Never, ever share a needle or works with anyone.** Once again, sharing needles or works with someone who has HIV is one of the most surefire ways to get infected. Remember, you can't tell who has HIV just by looking at him or her, and people who shoot drugs are at the highest risk for HIV. Assume that anybody who shoots drugs could be infected. Protect yourself!

Some clinics will give injection drug users clean, free needles so they won't be forced to use the same needles over and over again or share them with others. You bring in your dirty needles, and the clinics give you the same number of clean needles and destroy the dirty ones.

If you don't have a way to get clean needles, at least clean your needle and works every time before you shoot up. Don't use someone else's needle and works. To clean your works, you need some liquid household bleach, which you can get in any grocery store, and some clean water.

1) Put some bleach into a container. Fill your

needle and syringe with the bleach, then squirt it out. Do this three to five times.

2) Put some clean water into a container. Fill your needle and syringe with the water, then squirt it out. Do this three to five times, too.

3) Pour the used bleach and water down the sink. Don't use the bleach again.

4) Then take your works apart and soak them for a half hour in a mixture of bleach and water. Let them dry before using them.

Remember: Bleach three to five times, water three to five times.

Remember to clean all of your works, including spoons, caps, etc., by rinsing them in bleach and water. Hot water will **not** kill the virus. Always use fresh cotton every time you shoot up, and don't share water for cleaning syringes or dissolving drugs with anyone. You can also get bleach kits from some AIDS organizations.

When you decide you want some help, call this confidential hotline:

Center for Substance Abuse Treatment (CSAT) Hotline
1 (800) 662-HELP
Monday through Friday, 9 A.M.–3 A.M.
Saturday and Sunday, 12 P.M.–3 A.M. EST

"I have HIV."

bill Drumright was 45 years old when this interview took place. This is his story.

"I'm a native New Yorker. I have a middle-class background, middle-class ethics and ideals. I grew up in the late '50s, early '60s, during desegregation, and found myself the 'token black person' in school. There was a lot of pressure there, and I got even more pressure from the other black kids in my neighborhood. I just wanted to feel a part of everything, so I did stuff that everyone else in my neighborhood did, including getting involved with drugs: IV drugs, heroin, cocaine. Everyone I know shared needles. You'd get together at someone's house, and you'd just use the sharpest needle. We would clean it out with water, but certainly no bleach. I started having sex, but I never used a condom. I thought condoms would ruin the spontaneity. I carried one around in my back pocket for so long that when the time came to use it, it literally crumbled in my hands. I know now I should have used one."

Bill went to prison because of drug use: four drug-related felony convictions. He has spent most of his adulthood going back and forth between prison and addiction.

"I first learned about AIDS in prison, but in 1982 all they talked about was Haitians and homosexuals as high-risk groups. I wasn't in either of those categories, so I didn't think AIDS applied to me. Nobody was talking about AIDS and IV drug use.

"In October '89, I went into rehab. While I was there, I noticed I had a problem regaining the weight I'd lost through drug use. I felt weaker. I'd had a case of shingles. By that time, I'd read more about HIV, and a few of my friends had died from AIDS. After I'd been clean for four months, a counselor suggested that I get a physical. No one mentioned the HIV antibody test, but I wanted to know. The test came back positive. You'd think finding out would have sent me back into drugs. But I'd had just enough recovery to see that how I was living that day was better than how I'd lived the preceding day. I was building self-esteem. My sponsor told me to deal with it just like in Narcotics Anonymous: 'one day at a time.' I started going to support groups, and the first one was held in a hospital with all these seriously ill people with AIDS, people with IVs hanging out of their arms. I kept looking around and thinking, 'This is going to happen to me.' But then I started listening to what these people had to say. They told me, 'It's really not about dying of AIDS, it's learning to live *with* AIDS.' I still go to that group. And I've learned that the way to help others with HIV is to identify—not necessarily with their story, but with their feelings, what they're going through. We all have to find common ground.

"In a weird way, HIV has been a blessing in disguise. It's made me stop putting off for tomorrow what I could do today. It's added more immediacy to my life. I have a strong desire not to waste whatever time I have left, to leave some sort of legacy."

Part of that legacy is Bill's volunteer work teaching others about HIV prevention and helping those with HIV cope. He teaches them "to surround yourself with positive, supportive people. HIV is not the wrath of God. It's a disease like any other disease. As of today, it's a noncurable disease, but because you have it doesn't mean your life is over. None of us knows how long we have. Live each day as though it's your last, to the best of your ability." ∎

CHAPTER 6
if **YOU** or someone you **know** has **HIV**

what should I do if I have HIV?

i f your HIV antibody test is positive, don't panic. Your life isn't over because you have HIV. You've got to be strong, because tomorrow they may find an answer. Who knows? In the meantime, there's a lot you can do to give yourself the best chance for many years of healthy, happy life ahead. Each year that passes brings promising new treatments, more support services, progress toward a cure. Who knows when there might be a medical breakthrough? You are not alone; you're about to discover that there's a huge network of people and organizations all dedicated to helping you learn to live as normal a life as possible with HIV.

get into treatment right away

The earlier you're diagnosed, the better. There's still no cure for AIDS, but there are drugs you can take to help you recover from any symptoms you may be having, postpone others, and help you live longer and better.

Your doctor will know the best time for you to start a particular treatment. He or she also may prescribe medications to **prevent** some of the diseases you get when your immune system is damaged by HIV. Your doctor will advise you about covering the cost of medication. Ask for help, because the system of payment is different from state to state and even from city to city.

There are many different kinds of medications people with HIV can take. One type is the antivirals, so called because they fight the virus. Right now I'm taking an antiviral drug most often called AZT; the generic name is zidovudine. AZT works by keeping the virus from reproducing itself. There are other antivirals—both licensed and experimental. I don't want to get into too many specifics here, however, because treatment strategies are changing so fast that it's hard

about 1 million women each year are treated

to keep up, and some treatments are available only through clinical trials, that is, through places where the drug is being tested to see if it works. For the most up-to-date information, talk to your doctor or ask an AIDS hotline for information on treatment newsletters or other publications such as the Gay Men's Health Crisis's brochure "Medical Answers About AIDS." Join an AIDS support group and find out what treatments other members are trying. Educate yourself about your options and make your own decisions. Always let your doctor know of any drugs or treatments you are using.

More and more drugs to treat HIV infection are being developed and tested all the time. All these drugs can be used alone or in combination, which is why people who think they may have been exposed to HIV should consider getting tested. **The earlier you learn you have HIV, the earlier you can get treated and the longer you can expect to live.**

get in touch with the people you've had sex with or shared needles with

In most locations, the health department will do this automatically without revealing your name. If you've got HIV, I know how hard it is to trust society—and even family and friends—not to discriminate against you or reject you or isolate you. You might be tempted not to tell anyone you've had sex with or shared needles with that you've got HIV. It's your

for pelvic inflammatory disease.

decision. I believe it was my moral responsibility to tell the women I'd had sex with, so they could decide whether they should get tested, too. And think how hard it was for me to tell the whole world. It was really difficult for me to tell old girlfriends. But if I hadn't, I wouldn't have been able to live with myself. I felt I owed it to them for their health, too.

You might think, "Well, if there's no cure, why bother?" You should bother, because the earlier the others you may have infected—or who may have infected you—get tested, the earlier they'll get diagnosed, and the earlier they can get treatment and the longer they may live. Remember, you might get HIV and live a long, long time, but someone who gets the virus from you might die very quickly without treatment.

I felt I had a responsibility to do what I could to stop the HIV epidemic from spreading. The way I see it, if you don't tell the people you've had sex with or shared needles with, they won't have all the information they need to consider getting tested. They could go on unknowingly giving the virus to others, who will in turn give the virus to still others—and on and on, and more people—including babies—will become infected and could die from AIDS. Remember: You don't have to tell everyone yourself. Your health department or HIV counselor can usually tell people and still keep your identity confidential.

about 700,000 people each year are treated

take good care of yourself

Best advice: Get in contact with your local AIDS service organization. This is your best source for information, support groups, and advice on getting through the medical and social services system. Don't put all the responsibility for your health into the hands of your doctors; you can and do have some control over your medical care. Learn all you can about HIV and AIDS so you can work with your doctor as part of a team. Ask him or her to recommend a nutritious, healthful eating plan and exercise program —and stick to them. If you smoke cigarettes, try to quit. If there's a lot of stress in your life, find some person or organization to help you either get rid of the stress or change the way you deal with it. You can help get your body into the best possible shape and keep it there so you can stay well as long as possible. Learn how to listen to your body's signals so you'll be able to tell when it's time to get more rest, when you're under too much stress, or when you have a symptom you'll need to report to your doctor.

Let me tell you how I'm handling having HIV. I've got a positive attitude. I really think that's half the battle. My outlook on life is upbeat. I believe I'm no different from anybody else; I just happen to have this virus. I'm just going to keep going on with my life. I'm planning on living a long, long time.

Keeping yourself in shape is critical. I work out a couple of hours every day. Eating right is important, too. I've always eaten a healthful diet, so I didn't have

for gonorrhea, which can cause sterility,

to make too many major changes, but if you're not eating right, it's time to start paying some attention. Cut out the junk food, fried foods, and the extra sugar, and eat the most healthful foods you can find, including lots of whole grains, fresh fruits and vegetables, and fish, poultry, and lean red meat. Exercise and good nutrition can make a difference. Ask your doctor to recommend some good books on fitness and nutrition and some cookbooks.

get support

Learning you've got HIV can be very hard emotionally. It's normal to feel shocked, angry, depressed, panicky. You probably feel like your whole life has been turned upside-down. You might be afraid you're going to die tomorrow. You might want to lash out at the people you think gave you the virus.

When I learned I had HIV, I was disappointed, sad, shocked. Once I got over the first shock, I decided I would treat having HIV like I'd treated any other challenge in my life. I take that challenge seriously, and I'm going to face it with the help of my wife and my family and friends. I needed them to embrace me, to treat me the same way—and they needed it, too. And I'm going to keep right on fighting.

Build yourself a support system. I hope you have family and friends who can help give you love, strength, and support. You might want to try talking to others you trust, such as a member of the clergy,

arthritis, heart problems, and eye infections.

school counselor, or therapist. You might also want to join a support group so you can meet and talk with other people with HIV who can answer your questions and listen to your fears and concerns. Your doctor can tell you only so much, because he or she doesn't have the virus. The late Elizabeth Glaser, cofounder of the Pediatric AIDS Foundation, helped me out a lot. Only someone else with HIV can really understand what you're going through. Don't be afraid to ask questions of other people with the virus. Find your own strengths, and carry on.

Check the back of this book for phone numbers to call to hook yourself up with support groups and other services, or call 1 (800) 342-AIDS.

Remember: You're not alone.

HIV and your job

Discrimination against people with HIV in employment is against the law! If you feel someone is trying to discriminate against you in your job or at school because you've got HIV, contact a civil rights lawyer, the American Civil Liberties Union (ACLU), or another civil rights organization. Your state probably has a civil rights office that can advise you.

what should I do if I have HIV and get pregnant?

If you have HIV and get pregnant, the chances of your passing the virus on to your child are about 25 percent to 30 percent in the United States. That means that from 70 percent to 75 percent of children in this country who are born with an initially positive HIV antibody test go on to test negative for the virus within eighteen months and should then lead normal lives. Researchers are working on ways to prevent babies from being infected by their mothers, but no way to prevent this yet exists. They are also making progress on treatments, so be sure to discuss all of this with your doctor. A few children born with HIV are living and healthy so far at eight or nine or ten years old.

Since HIV appears in breast milk, your doctor will probably tell you that it's not safe to breast-feed your baby, so you'll have to feed him or her formula by bottle instead. (The World Health Organization recommends breast-feeding in developing countries, where there are no safe alternatives.)

HIV and blood, sperm, and organ donation

If you have HIV, the virus will appear in your blood, blood components, sperm, and organs. Therefore, you should not donate any of these. If you have already done so, you should tell the appropriate hospitals, blood-donation centers, and sperm-donation centers. If anyone received your donation, he or she deserves to know, so he or she can decide about being tested for HIV infection.

138

HIV is the start of the next phase of your life

Don't lose hope, and don't give up. You're still a normal person, and you can still do a lot of the same things you did before. Studies have shown that people with HIV who get treated early, take good care of themselves, and stay actively involved in the course of their treatment tend to live fuller, longer lives.

if someone you know has HIV
show compassion and don't judge

Try to imagine how you would feel if you suddenly found out you had HIV. Treat others with HIV just as you would like to be treated. Anyone with HIV or AIDS needs compassion, help, support, treatment, and preventive services—just like any other person who is sick or likely to become sick. No one deserves to get HIV or AIDS, and no one deserves to be treated poorly because he or she has it.

get over any fear of infection

You don't catch HIV through casual contact. You're at risk of getting the virus from an infected person only if you have unprotected sex with him or her or have blood-to-blood contact, such as sharing needles. Don't be afraid to shake hands with people with HIV or sit next to them on a bus, share a soda, play contact sports, work side by side, or kiss them. I've said it before and I'll say it again. Many people with HIV feel isolated and alone. People know when they're being treated differently. Don't be afraid to reach out.

genital herpes, which is incurable.

The only way a child could conceivably pass HIV to another child is if the child who is infected bleeds into the open wound of the other. But school nurses or staff take care of cuts and they know what to do, following universal precautions that every school has for any infectious disease. Children with HIV should be in school until their doctors recommend they should stay home. Any risk of infection is so small that we should all be prepared to live with it, because it would be so unethical to exclude that child from school.

Try to do whatever you can to end the ignorance about HIV and AIDS. Educate the people you know who don't understand how HIV is spread or who have prejudices about the people who get HIV.

what can you do to help someone with HIV or AIDS?

When someone you know has AIDS, you may feel helpless or useless. If that person is a relative or friend, you may say, "Just call if you need anything." More than anything, I just needed to feel like I was still my normal self. At the All-Star Game in February 1992, all the players came up to me and gave me hugs, kisses, high fives. They were telling me I was still one of them. It was the nicest thing they could have done for me.

Here are some suggestions that may help you to help someone who has HIV.

▶ Don't avoid your friend. Be there. It gives hope. Be the friend, the loved one you've always been, especially now when it is most important.

▶ Touch your friend. A simple squeeze of the hand or a hug can let him or her know you still care.

▶ Call before you visit. Your friend may not feel up to a visitor that day. Don't be afraid to phone again and visit another time. Your friend needs you and may be lonely and afraid. Bring a positive attitude; it's catching!

▶ Don't let your friend become isolated. Let him or her know about support groups and other services offered without charge by local AIDS organizations or hospitals, as well as opportunities for political activity or AIDS advocacy.

▶ Weep and laugh with your friend. Don't be afraid to share such intimate experiences. They may enrich you both.

▶ Tell your friend what you'd like to do to help. If he or she agrees, keep any promises you make.

If your friend is seriously ill, here are some more ideas of how to help:

▶ Call to say you are bringing your friend's favorite food. But ask to make sure it's something he or she is able to eat. Say exactly when you're coming. Bring the food in disposable containers, so your friend won't have to worry about washing dishes. Spend time sharing a meal.

► Call to find out if your friend needs anything from the store. Ask for a shopping list and make a "special delivery."

► Be creative. Bring books, magazines, taped music, a wall poster, or home-baked cookies.

► Bring along another friend who hasn't visited before.

► Volunteer to take your friend for a walk or an outing, but ask about and respect any limitations.

► If your friend is a parent, ask about and offer to help care for any children. Offer to bring them to visit if they are not living with your friend. Offer to take the kids to or pick them up from school or day care. Ask if you could make them lunch or supper or take them to the dentist, doctor, etc.

► Help celebrate holidays—and life—by offering to decorate your friend's home or hospital room. Bring flowers or other special gifts. Include your friend in your holiday plans. A holiday doesn't have to be marked on the calendar; any day can be a holiday.

► Send a card that simply says, "I care!"

► Offer to help answer any letters or phone calls your friend may have difficulty dealing with.

► Offer to do household chores, perhaps by taking out the laundry, washing dishes, watering plants, feeding and walking pets. But don't take away chores that your friend can still do. He or she has already lost enough. Ask before doing anything.

► Don't be reluctant to ask about the illness. Your

142 —————

friend may need to talk. Find out by asking, "Do you feel like talking about it?"

▶ Keep your friend up-to-date on mutual friends, other common interests, what's going on in the world. Your friend may be tired of talking about symptoms, doctors, and treatments.

▶ Like anyone else, a person with AIDS can have both good and bad days. On good days, treat your friend the same as your other friends. On bad days, treat him or her with extra care and compassion.

▶ Talk with your friend about the future: tomorrow, next week, next year. It helps to look toward the future without denying the reality of today. Don't underestimate the healing power of hope.

▶ Don't feel that you both always have to talk. It's okay to sit together reading, listening to music, watching TV, or holding hands. You can say a lot without words.

▶ Can you take your friend somewhere? He or she may need transportation to treatment; to the doctor, store, or bank; or perhaps to a movie or some other event. How about just a ride to the beach or the park?

▶ Offer to go with your friend to the social security or Medicaid offices to fill out forms.

▶ If your friend is a recovering alcoholic or drug user and can't get to his or her 12-step meeting, such as Alcoholics Anonymous, offer to call other people in the program and suggest they come to his or her hospital room or home for a meeting. If your friend is in outpatient treatment for drug addiction, he or she may need help getting to and from the treatment center.

▶ If your friend is concerned about his or her looks, be gentle, but acknowledge the feelings. Your friend may just need you to listen. Try pointing out some positive physical traits.

▶ Be sure to include your friend in decision making whenever possible. Illness can make people feel they're losing control over many parts of their lives. Don't deny your friend an opportunity to make decisions, no matter how simple or silly they may seem to you.

▶ Be prepared for your friend to get angry with you for no obvious reason, although you have been there and done everything you could. Let your friend get angry, but don't take it in a personal way. Remember: When a person is very ill, he or she often takes out anger and frustration on the people he or she cares most about, because it's safe and will be understood.

▶ If you and your friend are religious, ask if you could pray or attend services together. Don't hesitate to share your faith with your friend.

▶ Don't lecture or become angry with your friend if he or she seems to be handling the illness in a way that you think is inappropriate. Your friend may not be emotionally or mentally where you expect or need him or her to be.

▶ Don't confuse acceptance of the illness with defeat.

Acceptance may emotionally free your friend and provide a sense of power.

▶ Don't let your friend blame himself or herself for the illness. Remind your friend that it is germs—and germs alone—that cause disease.

▶ If you and your friend are going to have sex, be sure you know how to practice safer sex and use a latex condom and spermicide. Be imaginative—touch, stroke, massage. You don't have to have intercourse to have fun or be intimate.

▶ Check in with the people who are taking care of your friend. They, too, may be suffering and may need someone to talk to. They need a break from the illness from time to time. Offer to stay with the person with AIDS to give them some time off.

▶ Finally, take care of yourself! Recognize your own feelings and respect them. Share your grief, your anger, your helplessness—whatever emotions you may have—either with friends and loved ones or in a support group. Getting the support you need will help you help your friend.

"I have HIV."

elizabeth Glaser was 44 years old when this was written.

My name is Elizabeth Glaser. I am HIV-positive, and so are both of my children.

Three years ago, my daughter died of AIDS.

From my experience I have found that friends often don't know what to say when something scary or sad happens to someone they care about.

My friends who didn't call me after my daughter died, or after they found out I was HIV-positive, said, "I wanted so much to show you how I felt, but I just didn't know what to say."

For me, it was important to have friends reach out. All I really needed to know was that they were thinking of me . . . that they cared. That if I needed them I could call.

After that hurdle, I just wanted to be treated normally, sort of like anyone else. We all know my life is hard—but I don't want to have to think about that *all* the time and neither do my friends.

We can all take difficult situations and turn them into something that can bring hope and positive action. In my case, two friends joined me to found the Pediatric AIDS Foundation, which has brought hope to children and families with AIDS. I'm proud that I've been able to do something positive with a situation that seemed so full of nothing but negatives. ■

Elizabeth Glaser died on December 3, 1994. The Pediatric AIDS Foundation, an outstanding organization, is part of her legacy of loving and giving.

CHAPTER 7
if you're a
runaway
or homeless

e very year an estimated 1.5 million young people run away from home or get thrown out. Maybe you're one of them. You could be running from physical or sexual abuse or other problems such as a parent's alcoholism, illness, or neglect. Maybe you were kicked out—perhaps because you were on drugs or because your parents thought you were getting into other trouble or because you were gay and they disapproved of you. Or maybe you're running from foster care that wasn't working out.

It's sad that many runaways don't have a permanent roof over their heads and find themselves homeless, on the street, where they've got to scramble just to stay alive. If you're one of them, you know your life is hard:

▶ You don't feel you can turn to your families for help, since you're running away from home in the first place. And you might well be suspicious of any other adults or adult institutions, especially if your home life didn't give you a reason to trust older people. You might not be in school. You might not know where to turn for medical or mental-health services.

▶ You're probably angry, afraid, or depressed. Maybe you think the future is hopeless. Maybe you don't feel your life is worth anything—perhaps because other people told you you were worthless. **They were wrong.**

▶ You might not know how to connect with programs or organizations that could help protect you and get you back on your feet.

You're not alone. At the end of this chapter are some phone numbers you can call to get help.

protect yourself and your partner every time.

your special risk of getting HIV and other STDs

If you're a runaway and homeless, it's hard enough finding food, clothes, and a roof over your head. If you don't know where your next meal or bed is coming from, the last thing you're worrying about is developing AIDS five or ten years from now. But you should take this risk seriously. Being on the street may force you to do things that put you at a greater risk for getting HIV or other STDs. If you're depressed or suicidal, you might not even care about what could happen to you if you have unsafe sex or shoot drugs. Some kids find they have to turn to "survival sex"— prostitution—to get money, rides, a place to stay, food, clothes, or drugs. Maybe you turn to drugs— even injection drugs—because you think they'll help you get through the hard times or because they'll make you feel better for the moment. You might be drawn to neighborhoods where other teen runaways hang out, where you'll find kids having risky sex and shooting drugs and drinking alcohol. It might seem more "normal" to do these high-risk things.

I hope you'll get some help if you find yourself in any of these situations—please call the numbers at the end of this chapter—but in the meantime, here's some information you should know.

If you're selling your body to survive

Remember that you can get HIV by having unprotected sex with someone who's infected. You should act as though every person you have sex with could have HIV. It doesn't matter whether he or she got it from sex or sharing needles. **Practice safer sex each and every time you have sex—no exceptions, not even for the people who aren't your johns.** Use a latex condom (see Chapter 3) and spermicide each and every time you have sex. No matter how much someone pressures you or how badly you need money or drugs, **don't ever agree to have unprotected sex.** You can get HIV from having unprotected sex just once with someone who's infected.

If you do drugs or drink alcohol

If you do drugs or drink alcohol, remember that it's much harder to think straight when you're high or drunk. You're much more likely to take foolish chances and forget about using a latex condom and spermicide when you have sex. People who use crack are especially likely to take risks that could get them infected with HIV. No high is worth the trouble it could bring.

If you shoot drugs, remember that one of the easiest ways to get HIV is from sharing contaminated needles with someone who's infected. And again, if you're high, you're more likely to forget to practice safer sex. **Never, ever share your works with someone else.** Clean your works with bleach and water (see Chapter 5) before using them.

If you're a runaway or homeless, you have been

through a lot. You are a survivor; if you've left an abusive situation, you have already taken a major step to taking care of yourself. Reach out. Get help from a shelter or street outreach van or drop-in center. Protect yourself against HIV. You are worth it.

When you decide you want some help, call:

Center for Substance Abuse Treatment (CSAT) Hotline
1 (800) 662-HELP
Monday through Friday, 9 A.M.–3 A.M.
Saturday and Sunday, 12 P.M.–3:00 A.M. EST

If you go to a shelter
If you go to a shelter, especially one in a major city such as New York, Los Angeles, Miami, or San Francisco, you might find that some of the people staying there have HIV. Don't be afraid or angry. Remember: You don't get HIV from casual contact. Unless you have unprotected sex or share needles with a person who has HIV, there's nothing to worry about. You don't get HIV from anyone else's spit, sweat, urine, or stool or by sharing utensils or drinking glasses with them. See Chapter 1 for more information on how you do and don't get HIV.

If you're thinking of suicide
It's common for runaways to feel so depressed, overwhelmed, or hopeless that they think about committing suicide. If you ever feel you're on the edge, that

you have no friends, that you have nowhere to turn to, and that you'd be better off dead, call your local suicide-prevention hotline. You'll be able to talk to someone who really understands what you're going through. For more help, please call:

National Runaway Switchboard: 1 (800) 621-4000. The National Runaway Switchboard is a national toll-free telephone service that is open 24 hours a day to help you. Staff members provide confidential telephone crisis-intervention services for kids. They can place conference calls to your parents or deliver messages from you to your parents or guardians. They refer kids to shelters and other service providers and will place conference calls to these shelters and other agencies to help find the services you need.

National Youth Crisis Hotline: 1 (800) 448-4663. Open 24 hours a day

AIDS Hotline for Teens: 1 (800) 234-TEEN
This hotline is staffed by trained high school students. Call between 4 P.M. and 8:00 P.M., Monday through Friday, CST. If that line is not in service, call the **National HIV and AIDS Hotline at 1 (800) 342-AIDS.**

IYG Gay/Lesbian Youth Hotline 1 (800) 347-TEEN
Call Thursday through Sunday, 7 P.M.–11:45 P.M. EST

"I have HIV."

S.T. *is a middle-aged black woman who got HIV from someone with whom she'd been intimate for seven years. This is her story.*

To die or to disappear would be the perfect solution, or so I felt. I wanted to simply disappear. That would be the easiest, since I wasn't courageous enough to end my own life. The best I could do on that score was to contemplate the thought. After all, I couldn't stand pain, especially pain that was self-inflicted.

And so be it: my state of mind after finding that I tested positive for HIV eight months ago. My immediate reaction was one of disbelief and bewilderment. How could this have happened to me? Granted, since my divorce I hadn't exactly committed myself to a monogamous relationship (God knows I wished for one many times). I was single and had been for 19 years.

I had developed into a socially sophisticated, well-educated black professional and entrepreneur with high political visibility. I took great pride in the fact that I had always been very selective about my friendships and sexual partners. I was very much aware of the limitations surrounding love relationships with black men for professional black women. My intimacy group consisted of a "select few," which made the HIV diagnosis much more difficult to accept.

After the initial shock settled in place, anger marched in to engulf me to the very core of my being. Who did this to me? How could they without my knowing? When did it happen? Was I having an orgasm when "that thing" invaded my body?

I painfully acknowledged that I would not have known had I not acted on my desire to purchase an annuity insurance policy for myself and my only child. I completed the application and took the physical exam, only to receive a letter that I could not be insured.

After forwarding the results and hearing the news from my primary physician, I immediately rationalized, the way most folks would who profess to be normal: I was heterosexual. I'd always felt fairly safe and trusted the folks I was close to. I wasn't dealing with anyone new. Why worry, right? Wrong.

The virus had been passed on to me by someone I cared a lot about. Someone I'd been intimate with for seven years. And I was hurt and angry. Who would want me? I would be shunned, shamed, and considered a misfit during whatever time I had left, once my friends and family found out, right? Wrong.

I slipped into a paralyzing depression. I stayed in my bed as much as possible. I refused to clean my apartment, to cook, or to answer the telephone unless it was absolutely necessary. For three months I did nothing but what I thought was essential to my minimal existence. For three months I cried and couldn't tell anyone why I was crying or what I was feeling. For three months I felt as if I had slipped into hell. And because of that slip I had completely forgotten about the job and beauty of life and what I had accomplished prior to that time.

I had completely forgotten that I had successfully raised a beautiful son (now 22), gone back to school at age 26, graduated from a prominent university with a master's in public administration, and that I had successfully founded and implemented my own nonprofit organization. All I could see and feel was pain and darkness. And I didn't believe that I could feel any worse than this.

After I'd had enough of drugging and drinking myself into oblivion, and deciding that I couldn't stand myself in that state, I decided to reach out for help. I discovered that there is a happy beginning connected to that HIV diagnosis. I found a warm and supportive therapist who helps me deal with everyday stuff, one on one. I found a support group of women whose diagnoses were similar to mine, and we meet every week to discuss our fears, anxieties, and hopes. I found excellent medical care from three doctors who are accessible and have demonstrated a caring I'm sure most of us can say is never the norm among professional medical practitioners.

And my friends: God bless them. They have been so loving and supportive and I have yet to be rejected. That's not saying that I won't be at some point. It's inevitable given the hype and lack of information surrounding the virus. My biggest thrill, however, is that with the help of my support network, I am able to freely live . . . one day at a time.

P.S. Thanks to Magic Johnson, I recently took the step of speaking publicly, in the hope that I could educate others. ■

a final message from Magic

Take responsibility. It's your life. Remember: The safest sex is no sex, but if you choose to have sex, have safer sex each and every time. HIV happened to me, so I know it could happen to you. I want you to stay safe. Your life is worth it.

state-by-state directory of resources

if you were able to use only one source for getting information on any issue related to HIV and AIDS, it should be:

**CDC National HIV and AIDS Hotline
  1 (800) 342-AIDS
24 hours a day, 7 days a week
Spanish language: 1 (800) 344-SIDA
8:00 A.M.–2:00 A.M., 7 days a week
Hearing Impaired:
  TDD—1 (800) 243-7889
10:00 A.M.–10:00 P.M., Monday through Friday**

No matter where you live in the United States the hotline can direct you to any HIV- or AIDS-related service in your local area. This is a toll-free "800" number, meaning you don't have to pay for the call, and it will not appear on your phone bill. You don't have to give anyone your name. This confidential hotline can give you information about safer sex; how to find HIV experts to speak at your school; where to go for HIV testing; the latest treatments for HIV; or how to get legal, financial, medical, or psychological assistance if you are HIV-positive or have AIDS. The hotline can also send you free information about how you can prevent AIDS.

There are many other groups you can also call for information, and in the following pages, you'll find the names and telephone numbers of some of them. A complete list would fill a whole book. Although this is only a partial list, it includes many nationwide organizations and groups in or near your hometown that can tell you more about AIDS and STD prevention and treatment, help you sort out your feelings about your sexuality, help you get off drugs and alcohol, and guide you to food and shelter if you're homeless, a runaway, or in other trouble. Many of the organizations have toll-free "800" numbers for those calling from within the state.

You don't have to give your name if you call any of these numbers. The people at these organizations are there to help, and no one is going to judge you. Never be afraid or ashamed to ask anything; there are no bad questions.

You can also find resources through your local library or Red Cross chapter. The Red Cross can provide excellent brochures, comic books, and videos in English and Spanish on HIV and AIDS. Or if you're using the Yellow Pages, begin looking under these headings: Clinics; Family Planning; Family Counseling; Health Clinics; Social and Human Services; Abortion. Your state or city health department will probably have an office that can give you information about HIV prevention, testing, and treatment.

national organizations
HIV/AIDS Referral Lines and Hotlines:

CDC National HIV and AIDS Hotline: (800) 342-AIDS

AIDS Clinical Trials Information Service: (800) TRIALS-A

ACT-UP (AIDS Coalition to Unleash Power): Local chapters listed in your local telephone directory.

American Civil Liberties Union (ACLU) AIDS and Civil Liberties Project: (215) 592-1513

American Foundation for Aids Research (AmFAR): (212) 682-7440

American National Red Cross: (800) 26-BLOOD

Gay Men's Health Crisis: (212) 807-6655

National AIDS Information Clearinghouse: (800) 458-5231

National Institute of Allergy and Infectious Disease (NIAID) (301) 496-5717

National Sexually Transmitted Disease Hotline: (800) 227-8922

Pediatric AIDS Foundation: (310) 395-9051

People with AIDS Coalition of New York National Hotline: (800) 828-3280

Planned Parenthood: Look under "Family Planning," "Family Counseling," "Health Clinics," or "Abortion" in your local phone directory

Drugs and Alcohol:

ADAPT—Association for Drug Abuse Prevention and Treatment: (718) 782-2080

National Council on Alcoholism: (515) 244-2297

National Institute on Drug Abuse (NIDA Drug Abuse Treatment Information Referral Line): Hotline (800) 662-HELP

Minority Service Organizations:

American Indian Health Clinic: (612) 776-9519

Association of Asian/Pacific Community Health Organizations: (510) 272-9536

Bienestar: Gay and Lesbian Latinos Unidos: (213) 660-9680

Blacks Educating Blacks About Sexual Health Issues (BEBASHI): (215) 546-4140

Coalition of Hispanic and Human Services Organizations (COSSMHO): (202) 387-5000

Gay Mens Health Crisis—AIDS Hotline: (212) 807-6655

Girls, Inc.: (212) 689-3700

Lambda Legal Defense and Education Fund: (212) 995-8585

National Gay and Lesbian Task Force: (202) 332-6483

National Minority AIDS Council: (202) 483-6682

National Native American AIDS Prevention Center: (800) 283-AIDS

SCLC/W.O.M.E.N.: (404) 522-1420

United Migrant Opportunity Service: (414) 671-5700

Teens

The National Youth Crisis Hotline: (800) 448-4663

AIDS Hotline for Teens: Hotline (800) 234-TEEN (This hotline is staffed by trained high school students.)

Runaways:

National Runaway Switchboard: 24-hour hotline (800) 621-4000

National Youth Crisis Hotline: (800) 448-4663

state-by-state AIDS information organizations

The following list is a sampling of the AIDS/STD support and information groups in your area. If you don't live near one of the places on the list, call one anyway, and ask about finding an organization closer to where you live. Following each state name is a number for the state's own AIDS hotline, which you can call for local referrals. If the number begins with 800, it's a toll-free call, but can be dialed only from within the state.

ALABAMA:	**(800) 228-0469**
Anniston/Oxford:	**AIDS SERVICES CENTER**
	(205) 235-2437
Birmingham:	**BIRMINGHAM AIDS OUTREACH**
	(205) 322-4197
	JEFFERSON COUNTY DEPT. OF HEALTH, STD DIVISION
	(205) 930-1175
Mobile:	**AMERICAN RED CROSS**
	(205) 438-2571
	MOBILE COUNTY HEALTH DEPT.
	(205) 690-8167
ALASKA:	**(800) 478-AIDS and (907) 276-4880**
Anchorage:	**ALASKAN AIDS ASSISTANCE ASSOCIATION** (907) 263-2050
	ANCHORAGE STD PROGRAM
	(907) 343-4611
Fairbanks:	**INTERIOR AIDS ASSOCIATION**
	(907) 452-4220
Juneau:	**SHANTI OF JUNEAU** (907) 463-5665

ARIZONA: (800) 334-1540

Flagstaff: **COCONINO COUNTY DEPT. OF HEALTH SERVICES** (602) 779-5164

Phoenix: **ARIZONA AIDS INFORMATION LINE** (602) 234-2752

ARIZONA DEPT. OF HEALTH (800) 334-1540

ARIZONA AIDS PROJECT (602) 265-3300

Tucson: **TUCSON AIDS PROJECT** (602) 326-AIDS

ARKANSAS: (800) 445-7720

Fort Smith: **SEBASTIAN COUNTY HEALTH DEPT.** (501) 452-8600

Little Rock: **ARKANSAS AIDS FOUNDATION** (501) 375-0352

CALIFORNIA: Southern (800) 922-AIDS
Northern (800) 273-AIDS

Bakersfield: **KERN CHAPTER RED CROSS** (805) 327-AIDS

Berkeley: **EAST BAY AIDS CENTER** (510) 204-1870

Compton: **WATTS HEALTH FOUNDATION** (310) 606-0406

Eureka: **HUMBOLDT COUNTY HEALTH DEPT** (707) 441-5632

Fresno: **CENTRAL VALLEY AIDS TEAM** (209) 264-AIDS

Long Beach: **AIDS PROJECT LONG BEACH** (310) 434-4455

Los Angeles: **AIDS PROJECT/LA** (800) 922-AIDS/ (800) 553-AIDS TDD/TTY

CARA A CARA LATINO AIDS PROJECT (213) 661-6752
ALCOHOL & DRUG PROGRAM & ADMINISTRATION (213) 722-4529
MINORITY AIDS PROJECT (213) 936-4949

Oakland: **AIDS PROJECT OF THE EAST BAY** (510) 834-8181
AIDS MINORITY HEALTH INITIATIVE (510) 763-1872

Redding: **SHASTA COUNTY HEALTH DEPT.** (916) 225-5591

Riverside: **RIVERSIDE COUNTY DEPT. OF HEALTH** (800) 243-7275

Sacramento: **SACRAMENTO AIDS FOUNDATION** (916) 448-AIDS

San Francisco: **ASIAN AIDS PROJECT** (415) 227-0946
SHANTI PROJECT (415) 864-2273
AIDS HEALTH PROJECT (415) 476-6430
AIDS PROJECT/JEWISH FAMILY & CHILDREN'S SERVICES (415) 567-8860
LARKIN STREET YOUTH CENTER (415) 673-0911
OPERATION CONCERN 18th STREET SERVICES (415) 861-4898
SAN FRANCISCO AIDS FOUNDATION (415) 863-AIDS

San Luis Obispo: **SAN LUIS OBISPO COUNTY AIDS COUNSELING AND INFORMATION** (800) 590-2437

Santa Barbara: **SANTA BARBARA AIDS SERVICES** (805) 681-5120

COLORADO: (800) 333-AIDS

Boulder: **BOULDER COUNTY AIDS PROJECT** (303) 444-6121

Denver: **COLORADO AIDS PROJECT** (800) 333-AIDS/(303) 837-0166 TDD/ TTY

URBAN PEAK (303) 863-7325

DENVER AIDS PREVENTION & EDUCATION PROGRAM (605) 226-6625

Durango: **SAN JUAN BASIN HEALTH DEPT.** (970) 247-5702

Sterling: **NORTHEAST COLORADO HEALTH DEPT.** (970) 522-3741

CONNECTICUT: (800) 590-AIDS

Bridgeport: **BRIDGEPORT HEALTH DEPT./AIDS HOTLINE** (203) 576-7679

Hartford: **AIDS INFO AND REFERRAL LINE** (203) 522-4636 24-hr HOTLINE

AIDS HOTLINE AND COUNSELING (800) 590-AIDS

New Haven: **AIDS PROJECT NEW HAVEN** (203) 624-AIDS 9 P.M.–5 P.M. M–F

HISPANOS UNIDOS CONTRA EL SIDA/AIDS (203) 777-7411

New London: **NEW LONDON AIDS EDUCATION, COUNSELING, AND TESTING SERVICE** (203) 447-AIDS

Stamford: **AIDS PROGRAM/STAMFORD HEALTH DEPT.** (203) 967-AIDS

DELAWARE: (800) 422-0429

Wilmington: **PLANNED PARENTHOOD** (302) 655-7296

DISTRICT OF COLUMBIA: (202) 797-3500
NATIONAL AIDS MINORITY INFO AND EDUCATION PROGRAM (202) 865-3720
PLANNED PARENTHOOD (202) 483-3999
WHITMAN-WALKER CLINIC
(202) 797-3500/(202) 797-3547 TDD/TTY
SEXUAL MINORITY YOUTH ASSISTANCE LEAGUE
(202) 546-5911

FLORIDA:	**(800) FLA-AIDS**
Bradenton:	**MANATEE COUNTY PUBLIC HEALTH UNIT** (941) 748-0666
Gainesville:	**NORTH CENTRAL FLORIDA AIDS NETWORK** (800) 824-6745 or (904) 372-4370
Jacksonville:	**MAIN STREET CLINIC** (904) 798-4810
Key West:	**AIDS PREVENTION CENTER** (305) 292-6701
Miami:	**HEALTH CRISIS NETWORK** (305) 751-7751
	HAITIAN AMERICAN COMMUNITY ASSOC./MINORITY AIDS PROGRAM (800) 722-AIDS
Orlando:	**CENTAUR** (407) 849-1452
Panama City:	**BAY COUNTY PUBLIC HEALTH UNIT** (904) 872-4455
Sarasota:	**SARASOTA AIDS HOTLINE** (813) 951-AIDS
	COMMUNITY NETWORK (813) 951-1551
Tallahassee:	**BIG BEND/CARES** (904) 656-AIDS

| Tampa: | **TAMPA AIDS NETWORK** |
| | (813) 978-8683 |

GEORGIA:	**(800) 551-2728**
Albany:	**AIDS PROGRAM** (912) 430-5140
Atlanta:	**OUTREACH INC.** (800) 441-AIDS
	AID ATLANTA (800) 551-2728
	ATLANTA GAY CENTER
	(404) 892-0661 6:00 P.M.–11:00 P.M.
	7 days
	SCLC/WOMEN: NATL. AIDS
	PROJECT LEARNING CENTER
	(404) 584-0303
	TEEN CLINIC/TELFAIR COUNTY
	ADOLESCENT HEALTH SERVICES
	(912) 868-5152
Macon:	**MIDDLE GEORGIA COUNCIL ON**
	DRUGS (912) 743-4611

HAWAII:	**(808) 922-1313** 8:00 A.M.–8:00 P.M.
	Mon–Thur/8:00 A.M.–4:30 P.M. Fri & Sat
Hilo:	**HAWAII COUNTY DISTRICT**
	HEALTH OFFICE (808) 933-4708
Honolulu:	**LIFE FOUNDATION** (808) 521-2437
Kappa Kauai:	**MALAMA PONO KAUAI AIDS**
	PROJECT (808) 822-0878 24-hr
	HOTLINE

IDAHO:	
Boise:	**STD/AIDS PROGRAM** (208) 334-5937
Coeur d'Alene:	**PANHANDLE HEALTH DISTRICT 1**
	(208) 667-3481
Pocatello:	**S.E. IDAHO DISTRICT HEALTH**
	DEPT. (208) 233-9080

| Lewiston: | **NORTH CENTRAL DISTRICT HEALTH DEPT.** (208) 799-3100 |

ILLINOIS:	**(800) AID-AIDS**
Chicago:	**OFFICE OF AIDS PREVENTION** (312) 226-5864
	COOK COUNTY PRIMARY CARE CENTER (312) 633-3005
	STOP AIDS CHICAGO (312) 871-3300/ (312) 871-3300 TDD/TTY
	GAY COMMUNITY AIDS PROJECT (217) 351-AIDS
	HOWARD BROWN HEALTH CENTER (312) 871-5777
	MIDWEST HISPANIC AIDS COALITION (800) 542-1989
Decatur:	**MACON COUNTY HEALTH DEPT.** (217) 423-6988
Elgin:	**OPEN DOOR CLINIC** (800) 339-1093 or (708) 695-1093
Marion:	**FRANKLIN WILLIAMSON BI-COUNTY HEALTH** (618) 993-8111
Peoria:	**PEORIA CITY COUNTY HEALTH DEPT.** (309) 685-6181
	CENTRAL ILLINOIS FRIENDS OF PWA (309) 671-2144

INDIANA:	**(800) 848-AIDS**
Evansville:	**EVANSVILLE VANDERBURGH HEALTH DEPT.** (812) 435-5000
Indianapolis:	**INDIANA STATE BOARD OF HEALTH** (317) 383-6100
	DAMIEN CENTER (317) 632-0123
Gary:	**CITY OF GARY HEALTH DEPT.** (219) 755-3655

Muncie:	**DELAWARE COUNTY HEALTH DEPT.** (317) 747-7721
IOWA:	**(800) 532-3301**
Davenport:	**QUAD CITY AIDS COALITION** (319) 328-5464 6:00 P.M.–mid Mon–Sat
Des Moines:	**POLK COUNTY HEALTH DEPT.** (515) 286-3798
Iowa City:	**IOWA CENTER FOR AIDS/ARC RESOURCES & EDUCATION** (319) 338-2135
KANSAS:	**(800) 232-0040**
Lawrence:	**LAWRENCE-DOUGLAS COUNTY HEALTH DEPT.** (913) 843-0721
Topeka:	**TOPEKA AIDS PROJECT** (913) 232-3100
Wichita:	**WICHITA-SEDGWICK COUNTY HEALTH DEPT.** (316) 268-8401
KENTUCKY:	**(800) 654-AIDS**
Bowling Green:	**BARREN RIVER DISTRICT HEALTH DEPT.** (502) 781-8039
Lexington:	**AIDS CRISIS TASK FORCE** (606) 254-2865
Louisville:	**AMERICAN RED CROSS** (502) 589-4450 **COMMUNITY HEALTH TRUST OF KENTUCKY** (502) 574-5496 6:00 P.M.–10:00 P.M.
LOUISIANA:	**(800) 992-4379**
New Orleans:	**AIDS HOTLINE** (504) 944-AIDS **NO/AIDS TASK FORCE** (504) 945-4000

Alexandria:	**CENTRAL LOUISIANA AIDS SUPPORT SERVICES** (800) 444-7993

MAINE:	**(800) 638-6252**
Augusta:	**DEPT. OF HUMAN SERVICES** (800) 851-AIDS
Bangor:	**BANGOR STD CLINIC** (207) 947-0700
Portland:	**THE AIDS PROJECT** (207) 744-6877 TTY (207) 774-6877

MARYLAND:	**(800) 638-6252**
Baltimore:	**CHASE BREXTON CLINIC** (410) 837-2050
	CENTER FOR AIDS EDUCATION (800) 342-AIDS 24-hr HOTLINE
	BALTIMORE CITY HEALTH DEPT. (410) 396-1438
Salisbury:	**HEALTH SUPPORT MINISTRIES** (410) 543-1442
Baltimore:	**HERO (HEALTH EDUCATION RESOURCE ORGANIZATION)** (410) 685-1180

MASSACHUSETTS:	**(800) 235-2331**
Boston:	**FENWAY COMMUNITY HEALTH CENTER** (617) 267-0900
New Bedford:	**PROJECT CARE** (800) 696-AIDS or (508) 990-8280
Roxbury:	**LA ALIANZA HISPANA** (617) 427-7175 ext. 245
Worcester:	**AIDS PROJECT WORCESTER** (508) 756-5532/(508) 755-4084 TDD/ TTY

MICHIGAN:	(800) 872-AIDS
Ann Arbor:	**HIV/AIDS RESOURCE CENTER** (313) 572-WELL
Detroit:	**CHILDREN'S IMMUNE DISORDERS** (313) 837-7800
Grand Rapids:	**AIDS RESOURCE CENTER** (616) 459-9177

MINNESOTA:	(800) 248-AIDS
Duluth:	**GREATER NORTH AIDS PROJECT** (218) 727-AIDS
Minneapolis:	**ALIVENESS PROJECT** (612) 822-7946 **MINNESOTA AIDS PROJECT** (800) 870-0700 **NATL. NATIVE AMERICAN AIDS CENTER** (800) 283-AIDS

| MISSISSIPPI: | (800) 826-2961 |
| Jackson: | **MISSISSIPPI LESBIAN/GAY ALLIANCE** (800) 537-0851 24-hr HOTLINE |

MISSOURI:	(800) 533-AIDS
Kansas City:	**KANSAS CITY FREE HEALTH CLINIC** (816) 231-8895 **GAY SERVICES NETWORK/GAY TALK** (816) 931-4470 6:00 P.M.–mid
Columbia:	**MID-MISSOURI AIDS PROJECT** (800) 992-AIDS
Springfield:	**AIDS PROJECT** (417) 881-1900
St. Louis:	**METRO AIDS** (314) 658-1159 **AIDS INFORMATION HOTLINE** (314) 367-8400

MONTANA: **(800) 537-6187**
Billings: **YELLOWSTONE AIDS PROJECT**
(406) 245-2029
Great Falls: **NATIVE AMERICAN CENTER**
(406) 761-3165
Missoula: **MISSOULA AIDS INFO LINE**
(800) 662-9002 or (800) 223-6668

NEBRASKA: **(800) 782-AIDS**
Lincoln: **LINCOLN-LANCASTER COUNTY**
HEALTH DEPT. (402) 441-8000
Omaha: **DOUGLAS COUNTY HEALTH DEPT.**
(402) 444-6875

NEVADA: **(702) 474-AIDS**
Elko: **COMMUNITY HEALTH NURSING**
(702) 778-0780
Reno: **NEVADA AIDS FOUNDATION**
(702) 329-AIDS
Las Vegas: **WESTCARE FAMILY SERVICES**
DIVISION (702) 385-2090
AID FOR AIDS OF NEVADA (A-FAN)
(702) 382-2326

NEW HAMPSHIRE: (800) 872-8909
NEW HAMPSHIRE AIDS FOUNDATION (800) 458-AIDS
Wednesday evenings, 6:00–10:00, teen peer counseling/
teen hotline
GREENLAND FEMINIST HEALTH CENTER
(603) 436-7588
MANCHESTER HEALTH DEPT. (603) 624-6466

NEW JERSEY: (800) 624-2377

Jersey City: **HORIZON HEALTH CENTER, TEEN BEREAVEMENT GROUP** (201) 451-6300

Atlantic City: **SOUTH JERSEY AIDS ALLIANCE HOTLINE** (800) 432-AIDS

CAMDEN COUNTY HEALTH DEPARTMENT AIDS PROGRAM HOTLINE (609) 365-AIDS

New Brunswick: **THE HYACINTH FOUNDATION AIDS PROJECT HOTLINE** (800) 433-0254

Newark: **AIDS RESOURCE FOUNDATION FOR CHILDREN** (201) 483-4250

NEW MEXICO: (800) 545–AIDS

Albuquerque: **NEW MEXICO AIDS SERVICES** (505) 266-0911

NEW MEXICO AIDS PREVENTION PROGRAM (800) 454-AIDS

NEW YORK: (800) 541-AIDS

Albany: **AIDS COUNCIL OF NORTHEASTERN NEW YORK HOTLINE** (518) 445-AIDS

Bronx: **BRONX AIDS SERVICES** (718) 295-5598

MARTIN LUTHER KING HEALTH CLINIC (718) 681-3400

Brooklyn: **BROOKLYN AIDS TASK FORCE HOTLINE** (718) 783-0883

Buffalo: **WESTERN NY AIDS PROGRAM HOTLINE** (716) 847-AIDS

Long Island: **PEOPLE WITH AIDS COALITION/LI** (516) 225-5700

LONG ISLAND ASSOCIATION FOR AIDS CARE (LIAAC) (516) 385-2437

Manhattan:	**HETRICK MARTIN INSTITUTE FOR THE PROTECTION OF LESBIAN AND GAY YOUTH** (212) 674-2400
	THE DOOR: A CENTER FOR ALTERNATIVES (212) 941-9090
	PEOPLE WITH AIDS COALITION (212) 647-1415
	NYC DEPARTMENT OF HEALTH AIDS HOTLINE (212) 447-8200
	COMMUNITY HEALTH PROJECT/ HEALTH OUTREACH TO TEENS (HOTT)line (212) 255-1673
	GAY MEN'S HEALTH CRISIS HOTLINE (212) 807-6655/ TDD/TTY (212) 645-7470
	CENTER FOR COMMUNITY ACTION TO PREVENT AIDS (212) 481-7672
Syracuse:	**AIDS TASK FORCE OF CENTRAL NY** (800) 343-AIDS
Rochester:	**AIDS ROCHESTER** (716) 442-2200
Watertown:	**AMERICAN RED CROSS** (315) 782-4410
White Plains:	**AIDS RELATED COMMUNITY SERVICES HOTLINE** (914) 345-8888 TDD/TTY (914) 992-1442, extensions 250 and 251

NORTH CAROLINA: (800) 535-AIDS

Wilmington:	**GROW AIDS RESOURCE PROJECT** (800) 732-5461 ALIVE! for teens A good resource for lesbian and gay teens in particular.

173

Winston-Salem: **AIDS TASK FORCE OF WINSTON-SALEM** (910) 723-5031

WESTERN NORTH CAROLINA AIDS PROJECT
(704) 252-7489

Charlotte: **METROLINA AIDS PROJECT (MAP)**
(704) 333-1435 Hotline

Durham: **AIDS SERVICE PROJECT HOTLINE**
(919) 682-6066
OutRight (also in Durham)
(919) 286-2396

NORTH DAKOTA: **(800) 472-2180**

Fargo: **FARGOCASS PUBLIC HEALTH**
(701) 241-1360

Minot: **FIRST DISTRICT HEALTH UNIT**
(701) 852-1376

OHIO: **(800) 332-AIDS**

**THE LIVING ROOM/THE LESBIAN AND GAY
COMMUNITY SERVICE CENTER**

Cleveland: **HOTLINE** (216) 781-6736

DAYTON AREA AIDS TASK FORCE HOTLINE
(513) 225-5556

NORTHEAST OHIO TASK FORCE ON AIDS HOTLINE
(216) 375-AIDS

AIDS VOLUNTEERS OF CINCINNATI HOTLINE
(513) 421-AIDS

AIDS COMMISSION OF GREATER CLEVELAND
(216) 651-5001

COLUMBUS AIDS TASK FORCE HOTLINE
(800) 332-AIDS

OKLAHOMA: **(800) 535-AIDS**

OASIS RESOURCE CENTER/OASIS FOUNDATION
(405) 525-2437

174

Oklahoma City: **AIDS DIVISION, OKLAHOMA STATE DEPARTMENT OF HEALTH,** 24-hour HOTLINE (TTY/TDD avail.) (800) 522-9054

OREGON: **(800) 777-AIDS**
Portland: **PHOENIX RISING, GAY YOUTH SERVICES** (503) 223-8299
MID-OREGON AIDS HEALTH EDUCATION AND SUPPORT SERVICES (503) 363-4963
HIV ALLIANCE (503) 342-5088
BLUE MOUNTAIN AIDS TASK FORCE (503) 278-1529
Pendleton: **UMATILLA COUNTY HEALTH DEPT.** (503) 276-3211
Portland: **CASCADE AIDS PROJECT HOTLINE** (880) 777-AIDS

PENNSYLVANIA: **(800) 692-7254**
Philadelphia: **SPRUCE ADOLESCENT COUNSELING AND EDUCATION CENTER** (215) 748-0955
AIDS ACTIVITIES COORDINATING OFFICE (215) 875-5973
PITTSBURGH TASK FORCE ON AIDS (800) 282-AIDS
Wilkes-Barre: **PLANNED PARENTHOOD OF WILKES-BARRE** (717) 824-8921
Harrisburg: **SOUTH CENTRAL AIDS ASSISTANCE NETWORK HOTLINE** (800) 662-6080

PUERTO RICO: (809) 765-1010
PROGRAMA SIDA MUNICIPIO DE SAN JUAN (809) 751-5858

175

OFICINA CENTRAL PARA ASUNTOS DEL SIDA
  ENFERMEDADES TRANSMISIBLE (809) 721-2000
FUNDACION SIDA DE PUERTO RICO (809) 782-9600

RHODE ISLAND: (401) 277-6502
                     RI DEPT. OF HEALTH AIDS
                     PROGRAM (401) 277-2320
       Providence: **RI PROJECT AIDS** (800) 726-3010

SOUTH CAROLINA: (800) 322-AIDS
SOUTH CAROLINA AIDS EDUCATION NETWORK
  (SCAEN) (803) 736-1171
       Charleston: **COUNTY HEALTH DEPT.**
                     (803) 724-5800
       Columbia: **CAROLINA AIDS RESEARCH AND**
                     EDUCATION HOTLINE (800) 868-7257

SOUTH DAKOTA: (800) 592-1861
SD URBAN INDIAN HEALTH (605) 224-8841
RAPID CITY INDIAN HEALTH ADVISOR BOARD
  (605) 343-2368

TENNESSEE: (800) 525-AIDS
     Knoxville: **AIDS RESPONSE KNOXVILLE**
                  HOTLINE (615) 450-AIDS
PLANNED PARENTHOOD NASHVILLE (HAS
  SPECIAL GAY TEENS PROGRAM) (615) 356-5326
NASHVILLE CARES (615) 259-4866 (has teen volunteers)

     TEXAS: (800) 299-AIDS
     Amarillo: **PASO/PANHANDLE AIDS SERVICE**
                 ORGANIZATION (806) 372-1050
                 PLANNED PARENTHOOD OF
                 AMARILLO (806) 372-8731

Corpus Christi:	**COASTAL BEND AIDS FOUNDATION** (512) 814-2001
Dallas:	**AIDS RESOURCE CENTER** (214) 559-AIDS (HOTLINE) (214) 521-5124 program for les/gay teens
El Paso:	**SOUTHWEST AIDS COMMITTEE HOTLINE** (915) 772-3366
Houston:	**MONTROSE COUNSELING CENTER HIV/AIDS PROJECT** (713) 529-0037
Lubbock:	**SOUTH PLAINS AIDS RESOURCE CENTER** (806) 796-7068
San Antonio:	**PEOPLE WITH AIDS COALITION-HOTLINE 51** (800) 548-4659

UTAH: (800) 537-1046
UTAH AIDS FOUNDATION-SALT LAKE CITY HOTLINE (801) 487-2323
UTAH DEPT. OF HEALTH (800) 366-AIDS 24-hr. HOTLINE

VERMONT: (800) 882-AIDS
COUNSELING AND INFORMATION HOTLINE (800) 590-AIDS or (802) 254-4444
VT DEPT. OF HEALTH, BURLINGTON (800) 882-AIDS
BRATTLEBORO AIDS PROJECT (800) 254-4444 24-hr. HOTLINE
| Burlington: | **VERMONT C.A.R.E.S.** (802) 863-AIDS |

VIRGIN ISLANDS: (809) 773-1311
ST. CROIX-CHARLES HARWOOD CLINIC (809) 773-1311 ext. 3061

**VIRGIN ISLANDS COMMUNITY AIDS RESOURCE
AND EDUCATION** (809) 692-9111
WOMEN'S COALITION OF ST. CROIX (809) 773-9062

VIRGINIA: (800) 533-4148
FAN FREE CLINIC (804) 358-AIDS
**RICHMOND ORGANIZATION FOR SEXUAL
MINORITY YOUTH** (804) 353-2077
TIDEWATER AIDS TASK FORCE HOTLINE
(804) 583-1317
ROANOKE AIDS PROJECT HOTLINE (540) 345-4840
**VIRGINIA STATE HEALTH DEPT., BUREAU
STD/AIDS HOTLINE** (TTY/TDD avail.) (800) 533-4148

WASHINGTON: (800) 272-AIDS
SEATTLE AIDS SUPPORT GROUP (206) 322-AIDS
SEATTLE SHANTI (206) 322-0279
NORTHWEST AIDS FOUNDATION (206) 329-6923
RISE-N-SHINE (FOR TEENS) (206) 628-8949
SEATTLE AIDS PREVENTION PROJECT HOTLINE
(206) 296-4999/TTY: (206) 296-4843
**SPOKANE COUNTY HEALTH DISTRICT-AIDS
PROGRAM** (509) 324-1542
SEATTLE GAY CLINIC (206) 461-4540
    Olympia: **OFFICE ON HIV/AIDS** (800) 272-AIDS
    Ellensburg: **KITTIAS V COUNTY HEALTH DEPT.**
            (509) 962-7515

WEST VIRGINIA: (800) 642-8244
CHARLESTON AIDS NETWORK (CAN) (304) 345-4673
**CHARLESTON AIDS PREVENTION PROGRAM (HAS
YOUTH COORD.)** (304) 558-2950
HUNTINGTON AIDS TASK FORCE (304) 522-HELP
MID-OHIO VALLEY AIDS TASK FORCE (304) 485-4803

WISCONSIN: **(800) 334-AIDS**
Green Bay: **CENTER PROJECT, INC.**
(414) 437-7400
**MADISON AIDS SUPPORT NETWORK—THE HIT
SQUAD (FOR TEENS)** (608) 252-6540 24-hr. HOTLINE
MILWAUKEE AIDS PROJECT HOTLINE
(800) 334-AIDS (414) 273-1991
Wausau: **CENTRAL WISCONSIN AIDS
NETWORK (CWAN)** (715) 848-9060
Appleton: **FOX VALLEY AIDS PROJECT**
(414) 733-2068

WYOMING: **(800) 327-3577**
Casper: **WYOMING AIDS PROJECT**
(800) 635-2698 24-hr. HOTLINE

Canadian resources

NATIONAL AIDS ORGANIZATIONS
Bureau of HIV/AIDS/STDs (613) 957-1777
Canadian Public Health Association (613) 725-3434
Canadian AIDS Society (613) 230-3580
Canadian Hemophilia Society (514) 848-0503

YUKON
Communicable Disease Control (403) 667-8323
Yukon AIDS Program (800) 661-0507

NORTHWEST TERRITORIES
Information Hot Line (800) 661-0795

BRITISH COLUMBIA
British Columbia Information Hot Line (800) 972-AIDS

Vancouver
AIDS Vancouver Help Line (604) 687-AIDS
British Columbia PWA Society (604) 681-2122
Positive Women's Network (604) 681-2122

Victoria
AIDS Vancouver Island (604) 384-2366

ALBERTA
Information Hot Line (800) 772-AIDS

Calgary
AIDS Calgary (403) 228-0155

Edmonton

AIDS Network of Edmonton   (403) 488-5816

Edmonton Persons Living with HIV Society/Living Positive
   (403) 488-5768

Feather of Hope Aboriginal AIDS Prevention Society
   (800) 256-0459 or (403) 488-5773

Red Deer

Central Alberta AIDS Network   (403) 346-8858

SASKATCHEWAN

Information Hot Line   (800) 667-6876

Regina

AIDS Regina   (306) 924-8420

Saskatoon

AIDS Saskatoon   (306) 242-5005

Gay and Lesbian Health Services   (306) 665-1224

PLWA Network of Saskatchewan   (306) 373-7766

MANITOBA

Information Hot Line   (800) 782-AIDS

Winnipeg

AIDS/STD Information Line   (204) 945-AIDS

AIDS Shelter Coalition of Manitoba   (204) 775-9173

Village Clinic   (204) 453-0045

ONTARIO

Information Hot Line (English/French)   (800) 267-7432

Sex Information Hot Line   (800) 463-6739

Hamilton

Hamilton AIDS Network   (905) 528-0854

Kingston

Kingston AIDS Project   (613) 545-3698

Kitchener

AIDS Committee of Cambridge, Kitchener, Waterloo, and
  Area   (519) 570-3687

London

AIDS Committee of London   (519) 434-1601

North Bay

AIDS Committee of North Bay and Area   (705) 497-3560

Ottawa

AIDS Committee of Ottawa   (613) 238-5014
AIDS Housing Group of Ottawa   (613) 235-8815

St. Catharines

AIDS Niagara   (905) 984-8684

Sudbury

Access: The AIDS Committee of Sudbury   (705) 688-0505

Thunder Bay

AIDS Committee of Thunder Bay   (807) 345-1516

Toronto

AIDS Committee of Toronto   (416) 340-AIDS
Alliance for South Asian AIDS Prevention   (416) 351-0131
Black Coalition for AIDS Prevention   (416) 926-0122
Casey House Hospice   (416) 962-7600
Community AIDS Treatment Information Exchange   (416)
  928-2206

Prostitutes' Safe Sex Project   (416) 964-0150
Toronto People With AIDS Foundation   (416) 506-1400

Windsor
AIDS Committee of Windsor   (519) 973-0222

QUEBEC
Information Hot Line   (800) 463-5656

Montreal
AIDS Community Care Montreal   (514) 939-0075

NEW BRUNSWICK
Information Hot Line   (800) 561-4009 or (506) 459-7518

Moncton
AIDS Moncton   (506) 859-9616

Saint John
AIDS Saint John   (506) 652-2437

NOVA SCOTIA
Information Hot Line   (800) 566-AIDS

Halifax
AIDS Coalition of Nova Scotia   (902) 425-4882

PRINCE EDWARD ISLAND
Information Hot Line   (800) 314-AIDS

Charlottetown
AIDS P.E.I.   (902) 566-2437

NEWFOUNDLAND

Information Hot Line   (800) 563-1575
For Labrador, Newfoundland, and St. John's

St. John's
Newfoundland AIDS Committee   (709) 579-8656

index

Numerals in *italics* indicate illustrations.

about the author

Earvin "MAGIC" Johnson, a three-time win-
ner of the NBA's Most Valuable Player Award, led the
Los Angeles Lakers to five world championships. He
is the founder of the Magic Johnson Foundation,
which is dedicated to HIV/AIDS education, prevention, and care.